RENT
EASY PIANO

Cover photos: Amy Guip

Interior photos: Joan Marcus

ISBN 978-0-7935-7903-7

HAL•LEONARD®
CORPORATION
7777 W. BLUEMOUND RD. P.O. BOX 13819 MILWAUKEE, WI 53213

Visit Hal Leonard Online at
www.halleonard.com

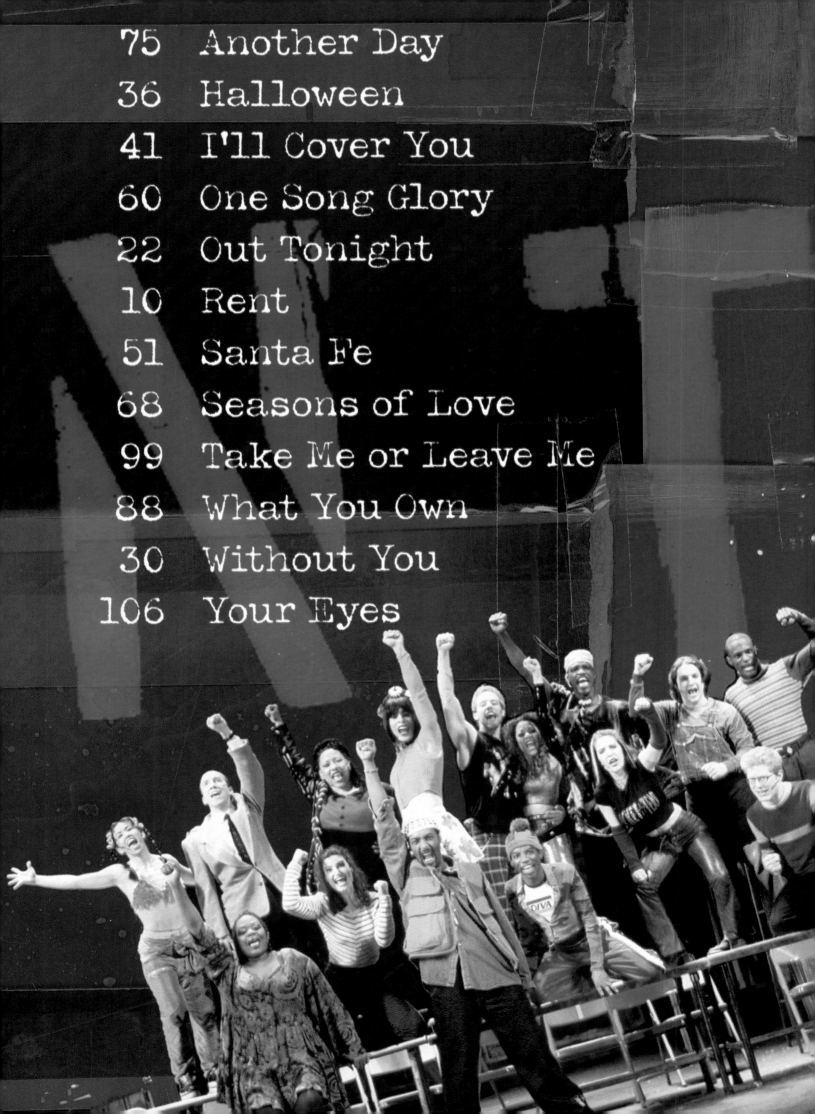

Jonathan Larson

February 4, 1960 - January 25, 1996

Jonathan Larson spent the greater part of his life working toward success in the theater. For most of his last fourteen years, he supported himself as a waiter while struggling to combine modern music with the drama of live theater; theater that would appeal to his generation and to those that would follow. While he had plans for much more, RENT was the culmination of those efforts.

Photo: Richard Lee

Jonathan did not live to see RENT open Off Broadway. He did not read the rave reviews or see the limousines lined up in front of the small theater...did not watch his show move to Broadway and to theaters around the country...was not able to accept the Pulitzer Prize and Tony® Awards he earned or to revel in the presence of a Broadway audience that was joyously yelling and applauding.

He never had the pleasure of being engulfed in the electrifying excitement that is present when RENT is on the stage.

His sudden, unexpected death on the day before his dream came true is the stuff of tragedy.

But Jonathan's was a magnificent talent and he left us a magnificent gift. He left us a show that is of our time — and of all time. A show that speaks in both words and music to the specific issues of today and to the timeless problems that humankind has faced through all eternity. A show that gives us another way to look at things. A show that teaches love — not fear.

It is an enormous gift which, happily, is reaching, touching and changing thousands of lives.

It is his legacy; his gift to us and to our children and to our children's children. Enjoy it.

RENT

Words and Music by
JONATHAN LARSON

Bright Rock

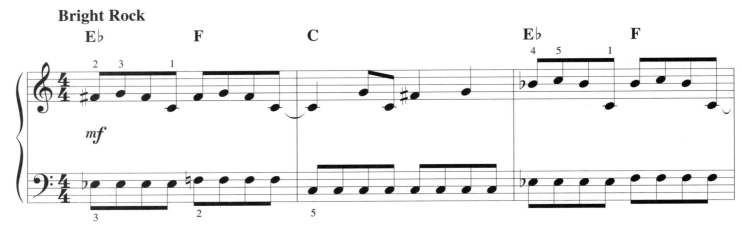

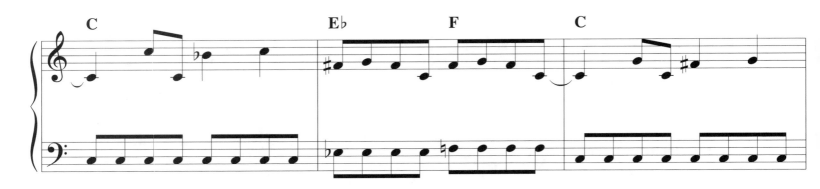

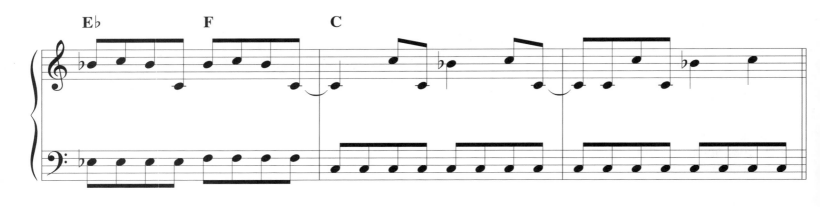

How do you doc - u - ment real life when real life's

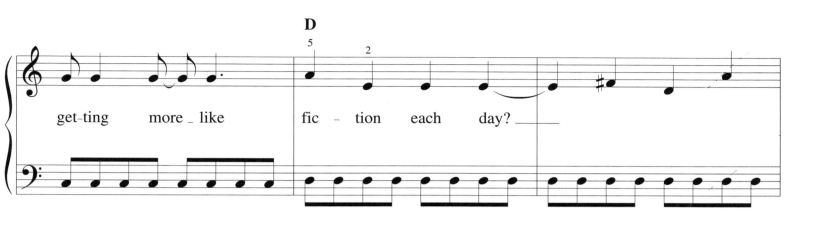

get-ting more _ like fic – tion each day? ____

Head – lines, bread lines, blow my mind _ and now ____ this dead – line, e –

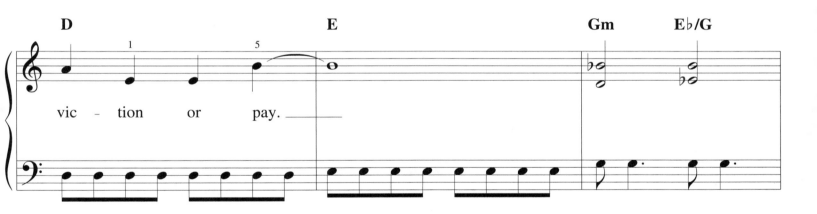

vic – tion or pay. ____

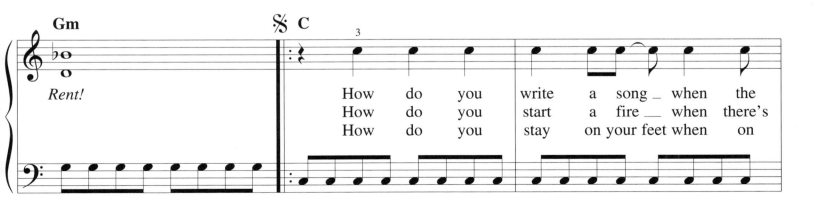

Rent!

How do you write a song _ when the
How do you start a fire _ when there's
How do you stay on your feet when on

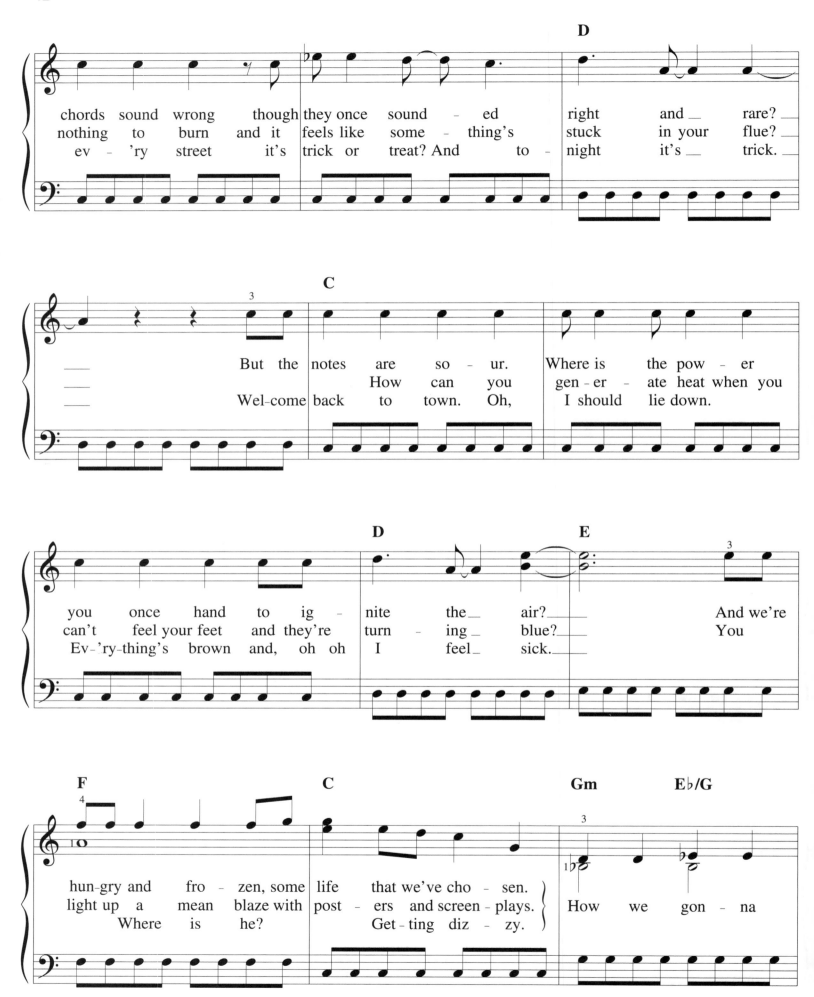

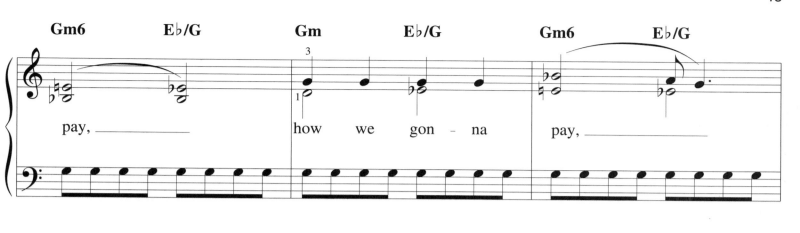

pay, _____ how we gon - na pay, _____

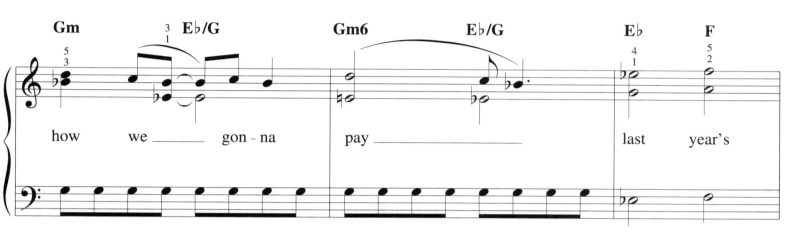

how we _____ gon - na pay _____ last year's

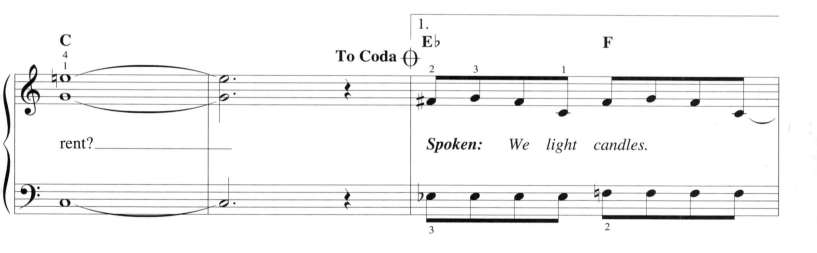

rent? _____ **Spoken:** *We light candles.*

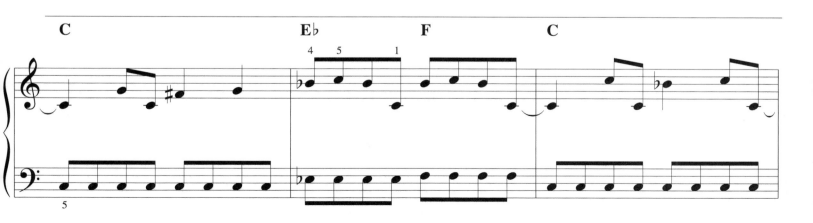

2.

C7

Spoken: Don't scream, Maureen. It's me, Joanne, your substitute

N.C.   **C7**

production   manager.   *Hey, hey, hey! Did* you   eat?   **Sung:** Don't change the

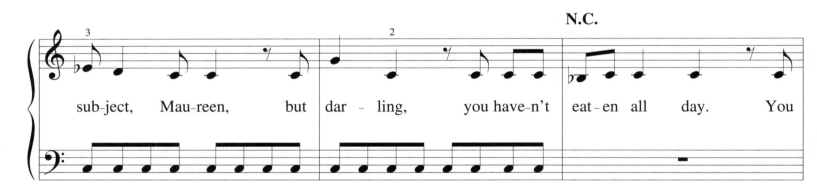

N.C.

sub-ject, Mau-reen,   but   dar – ling,   you have-n't   eat-en   all   day.   You

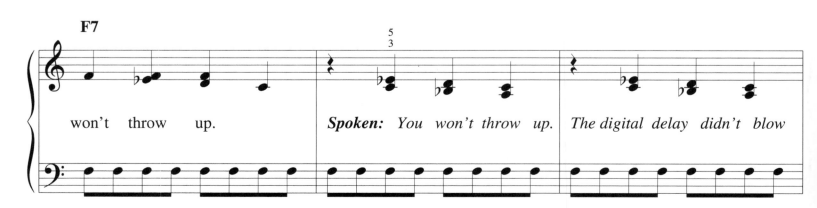

F7

won't   throw   up.   *Spoken: You won't throw up.*   *The digital delay didn't blow*

up exactly.   There   may   have   been   one   teeny,   tiny   spark.

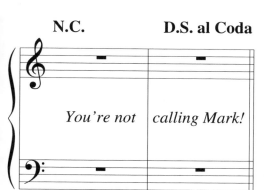

You're not | calling Mark!

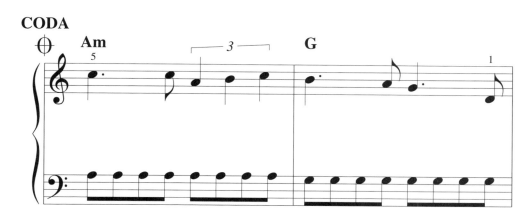

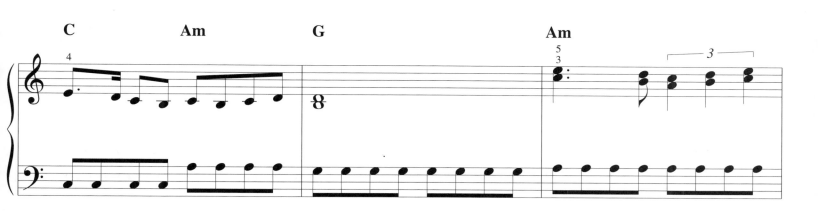

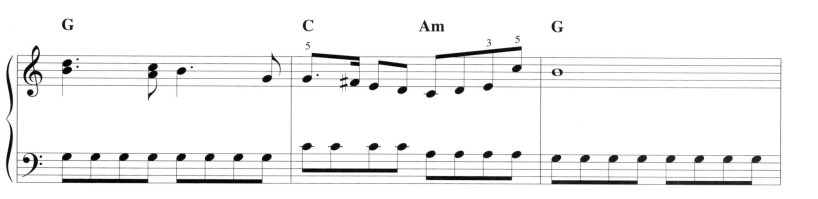

Al - i - son, ba - by, **Spoken:** *you sound sad. I don't believe those two after*

everything I've done. Ever since our wedding I'm dirt. They'll see Joan

help them all out in the long run. **Sung:** The mu - sic ig -

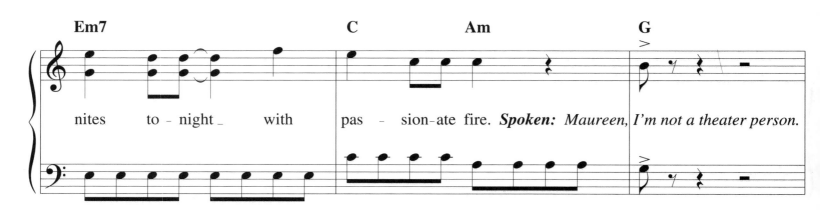

nites to - night_ with pas - sion-ate fire. **Spoken:** *Maureen, I'm not a theater person.*

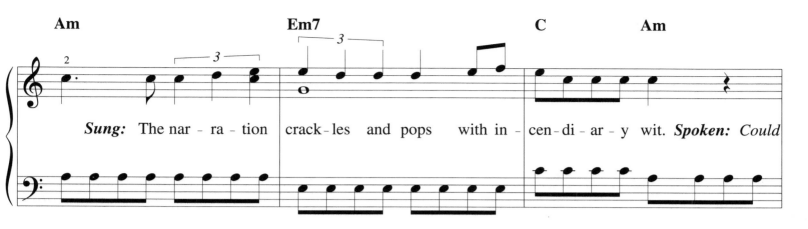

Sung: The nar - ra - tion crack - les and pops with in - cen - di - ar - y wit. *Spoken: Could*

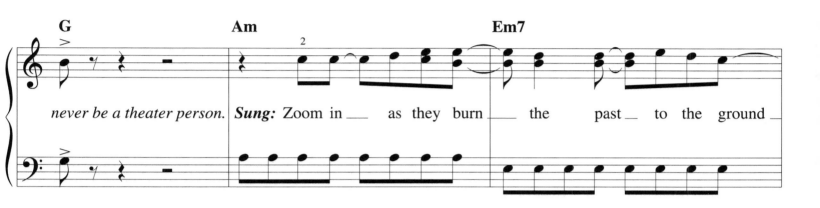

never be a theater person. **Sung:** Zoom in ___ as they burn ___ the past ___ to the ground ___

___ and I'm feel - ing the heat ___ of the fu - ture's glow. ___ **Spoken:** *Hello, hello?*

Maureen?   Your   equipment   won't   work?   Okay,   alright,   I'll   go!

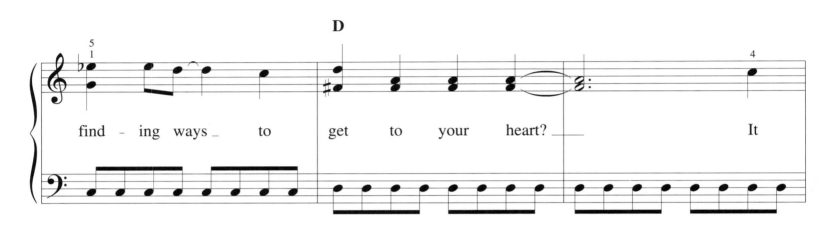

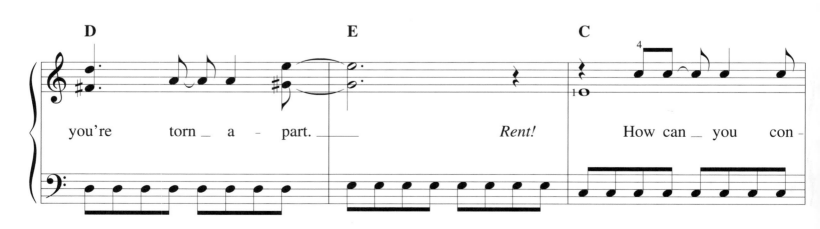

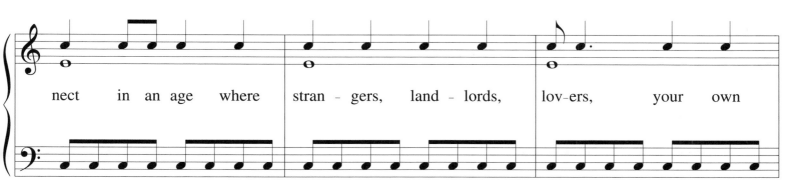

nect in an age where stran - gers, land - lords, lov-ers, your own

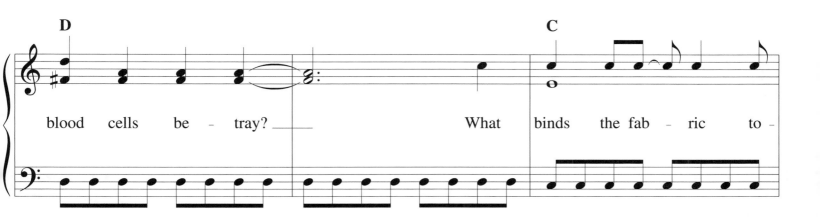

blood cells be - tray? ___ What binds the fab - ric to -

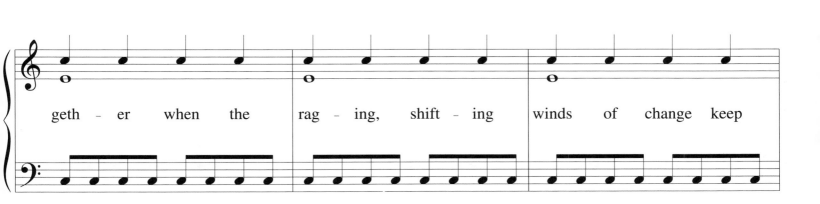

geth - er when the rag - ing, shift - ing winds of change keep

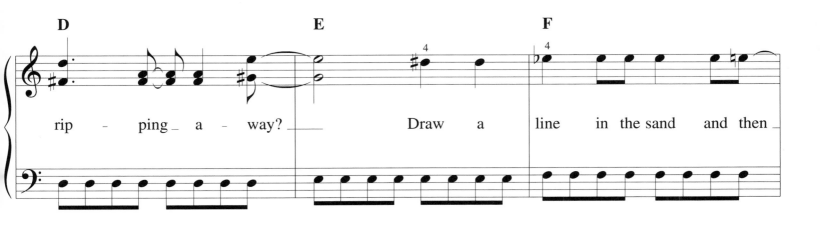

rip - ping _ a - way? ___ Draw a line in the sand and then _

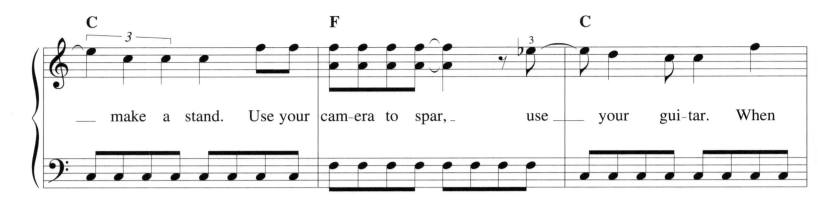

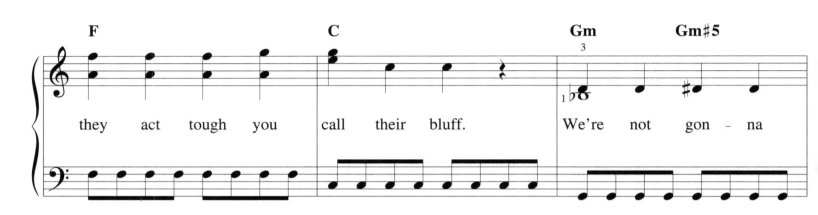

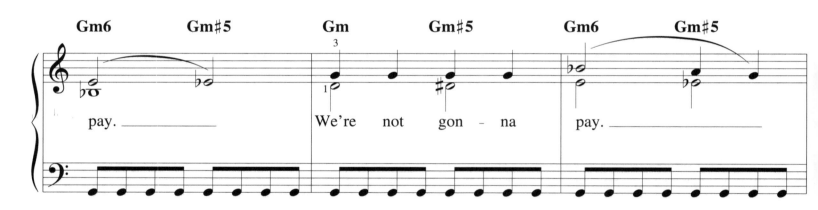

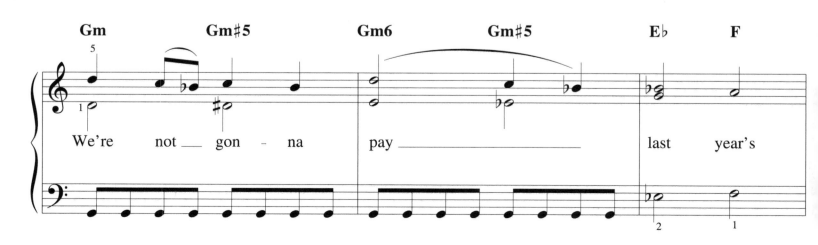

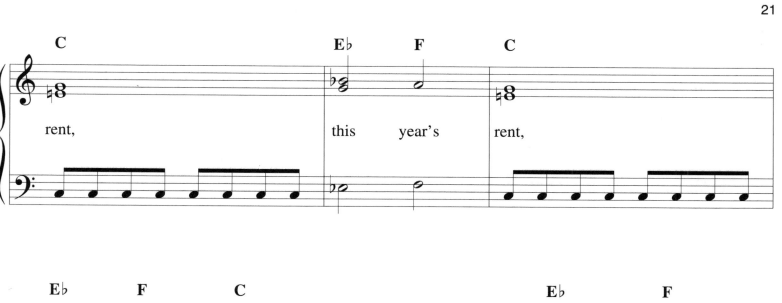

rent,   this year's rent,

next year's rent.   Rent, rent, rent, rent, ___

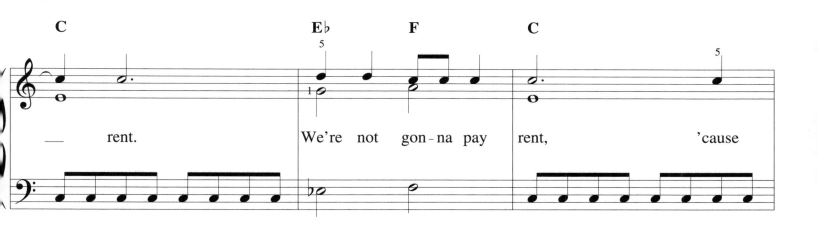

___ rent.   We're not gon - na pay rent, 'cause

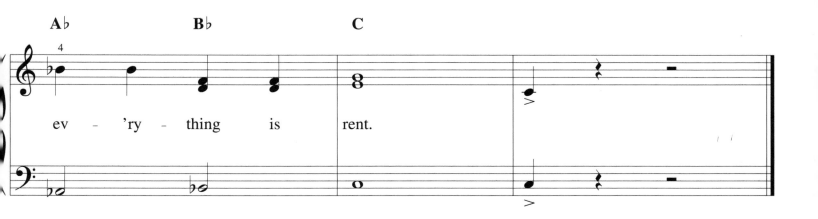

ev - 'ry - thing is rent.

OUT TONIGHT

Words and Music by
JONATHAN LARSON

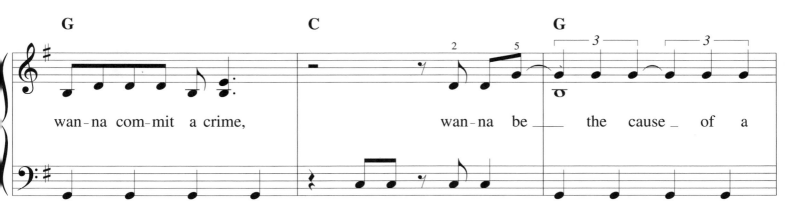

wan-na com-mit a crime,   wan-na be   the cause _ of a

fight.   I wan-na put on a ___ tight skirt ___ and flirt with a

stran - ger."   I've had a knack   from _

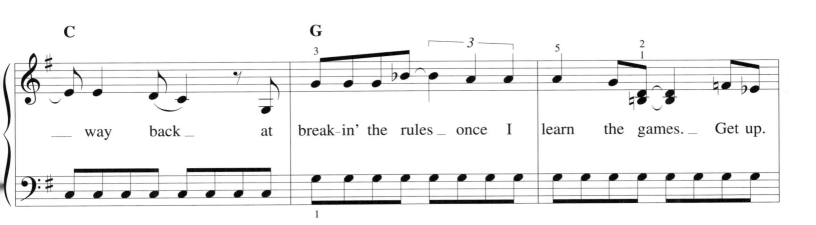

_ way back _ at break-in' the rules _ once I learn the games. _ Get up.

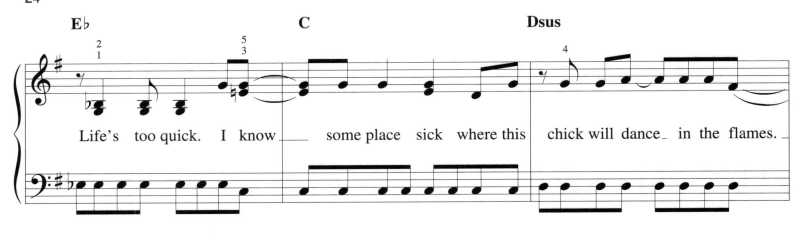

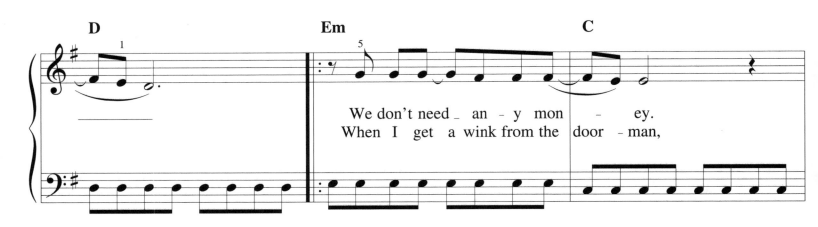

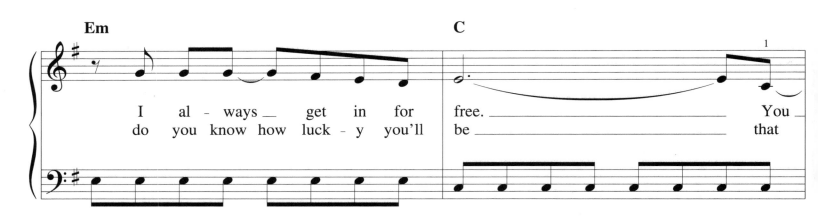

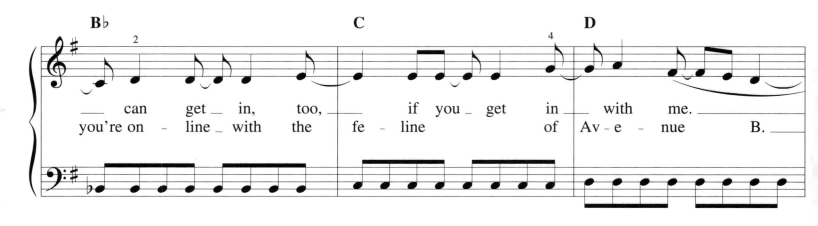

Christ - mas Day. ____ Take me out ____ to - night. ____

Me - ow!

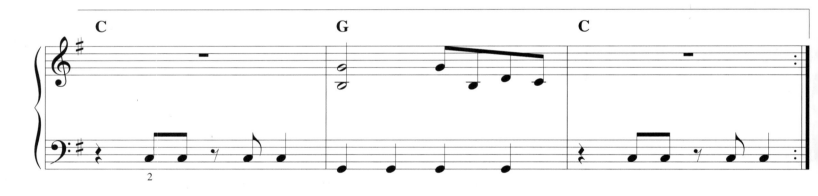

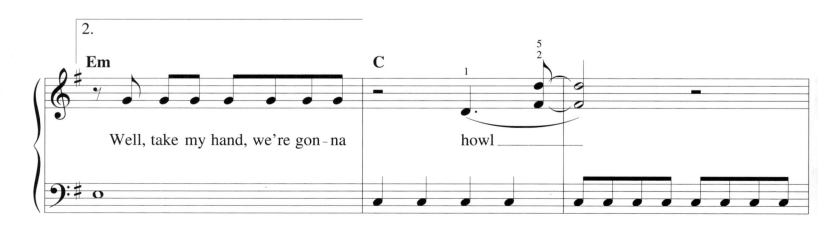

2.

Well, take my hand, we're gon - na howl _____

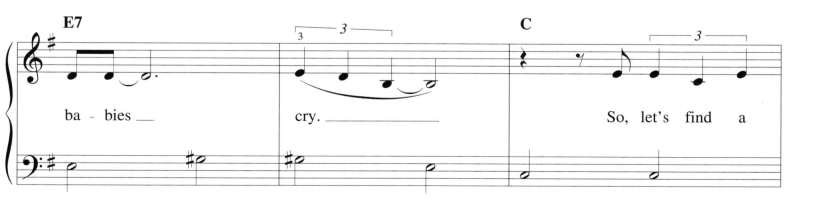

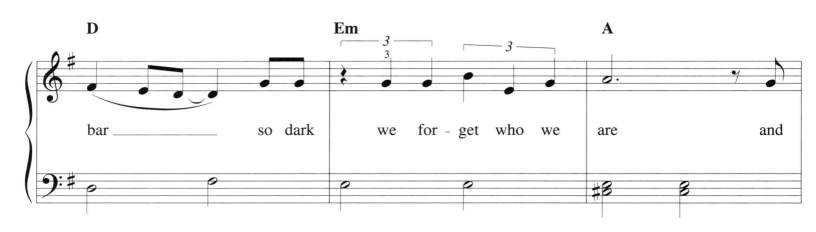

bar _____ so dark we for-get who we are and

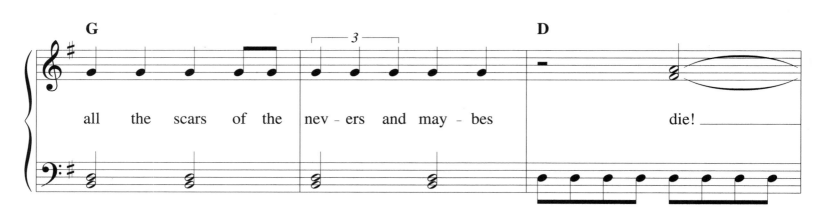

all the scars of the nev-ers and may-bes die! _____

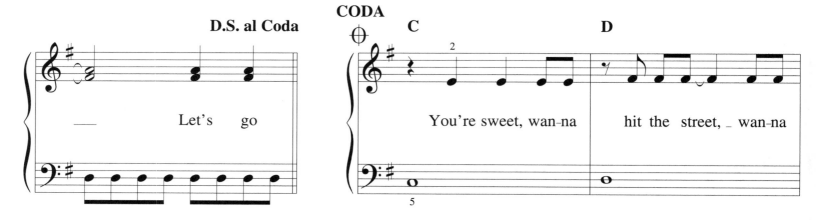

D.S. al Coda   **CODA**

_____ Let's go   You're sweet, wan-na hit the street, _ wan-na

wail at the moon _ like a cat ___ in heat. _ Just take me _____ out

WITHOUT YOU

Words and Music by
JONATHAN LARSON

Moderately flowing

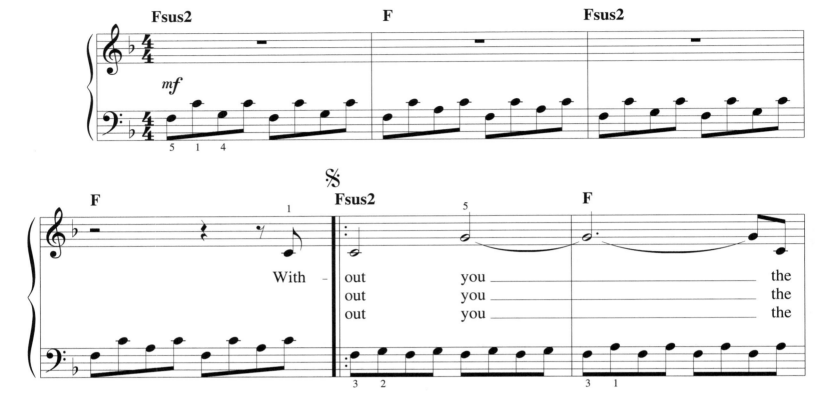

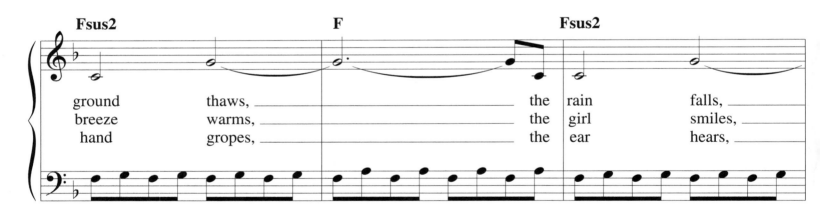

ground	thaws,	the rain falls,
breeze	warms,	the girl smiles,
hand	gropes,	the ear hears,

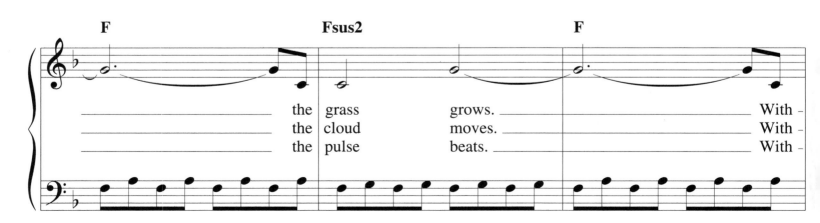

the grass	grows.	With -
the cloud	moves.	With -
the pulse	beats.	With -

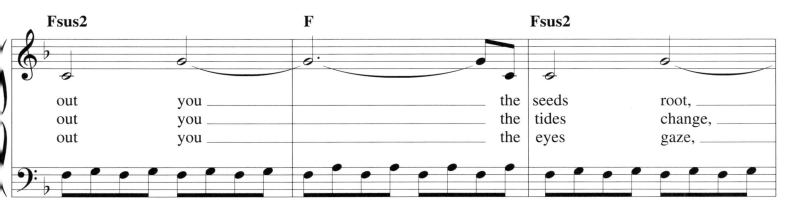

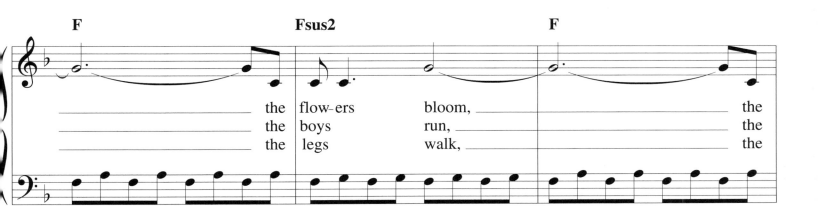

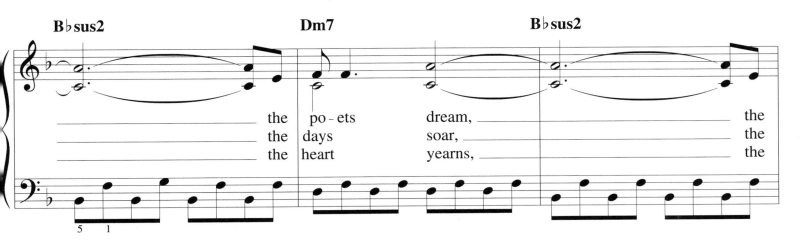

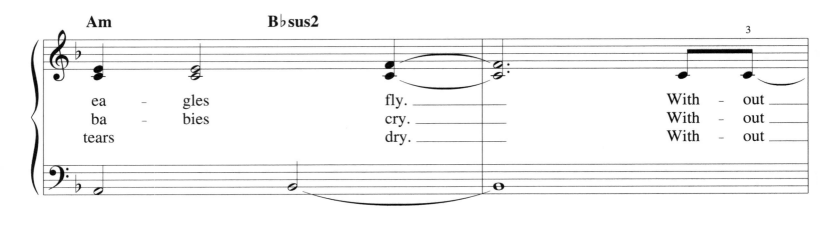

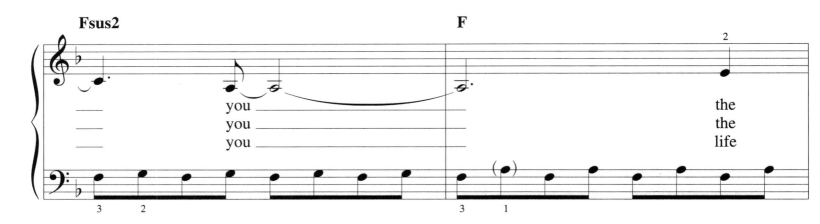

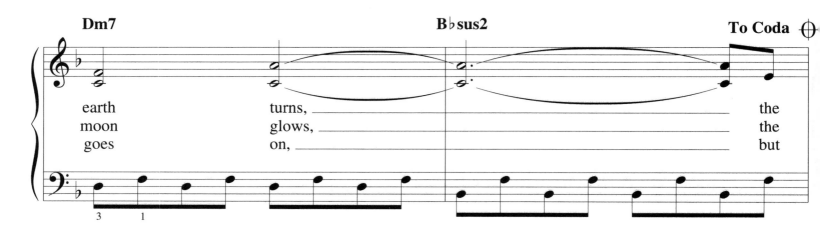

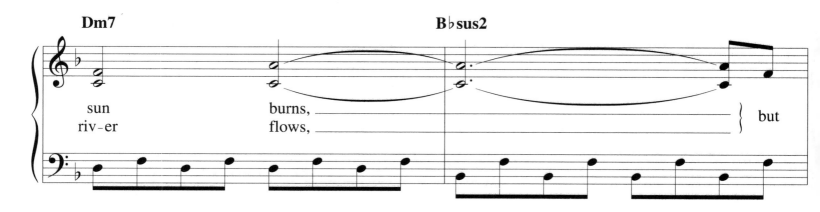

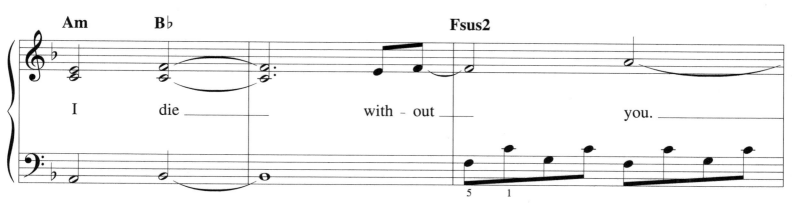

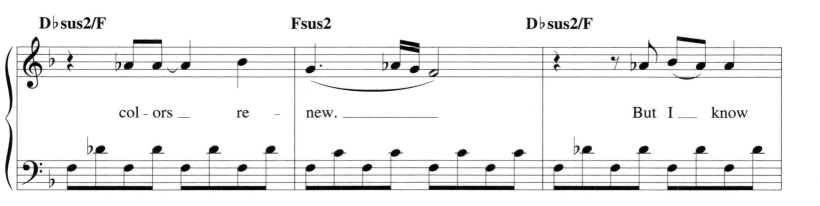

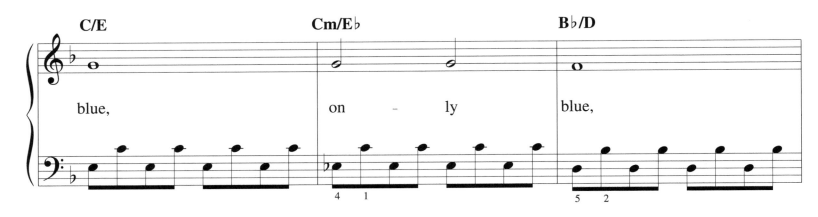

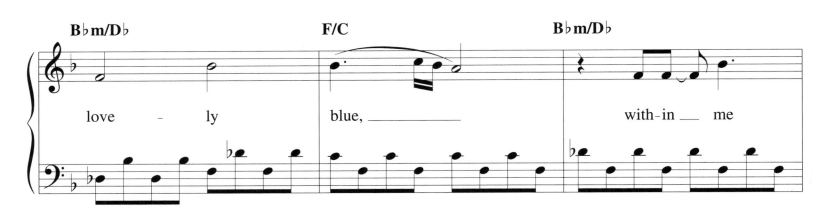

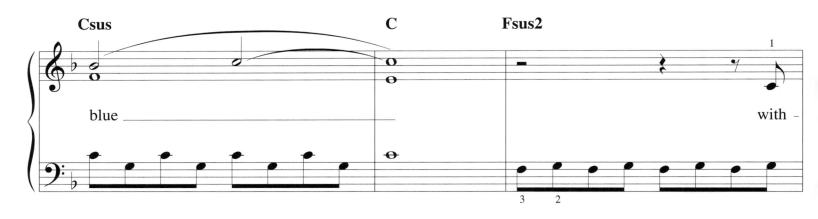

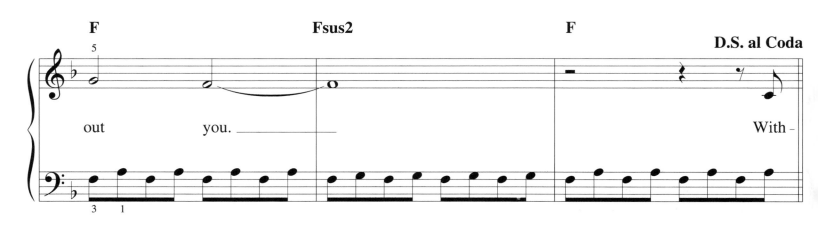

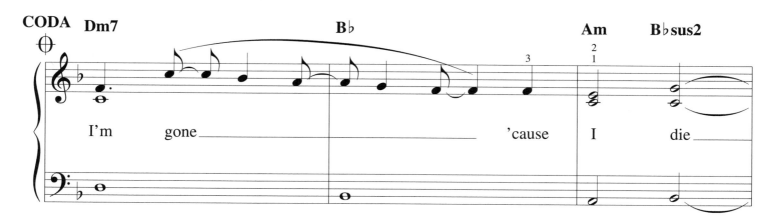

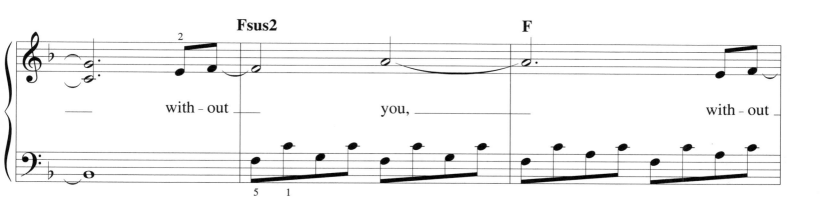

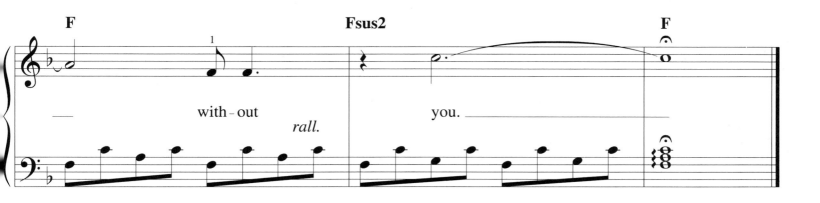

HALLOWEEN

Words and Music by
JONATHAN LARSON

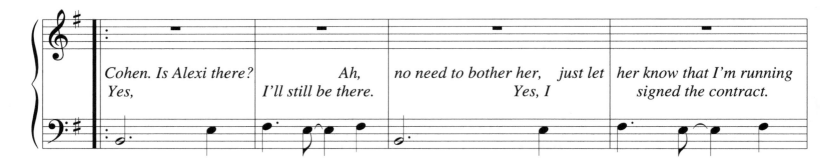

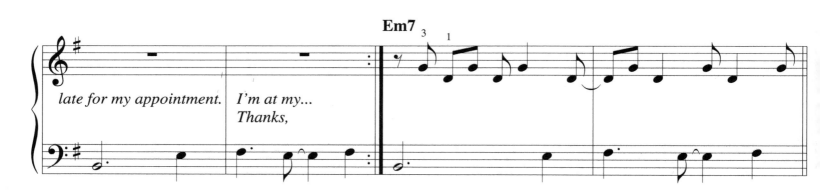

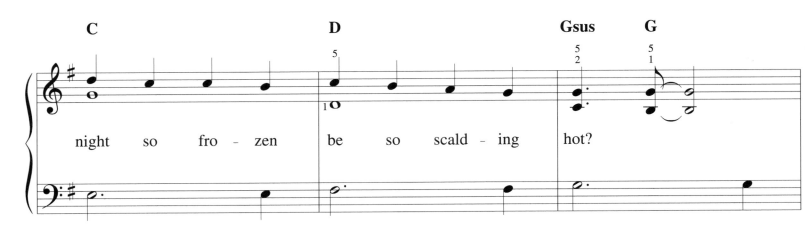

night so fro – zen   be so scald – ing   hot?

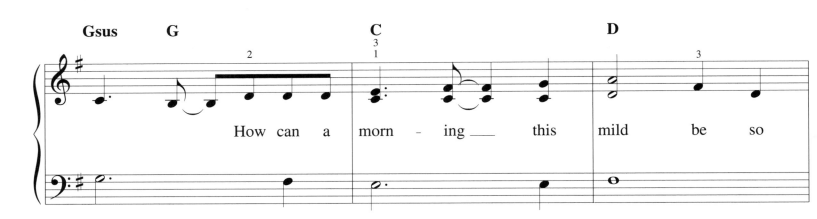

How can a morn – ing ____ this   mild be so

raw?   Why are en – ti – re years

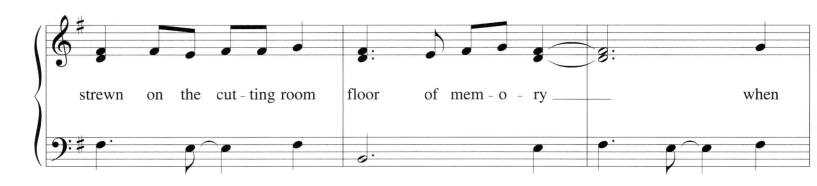

strewn on the cut – ting room   floor of mem – o – ry _____   when

single frames _ from one mag - ic night for - ev - er flick - er in

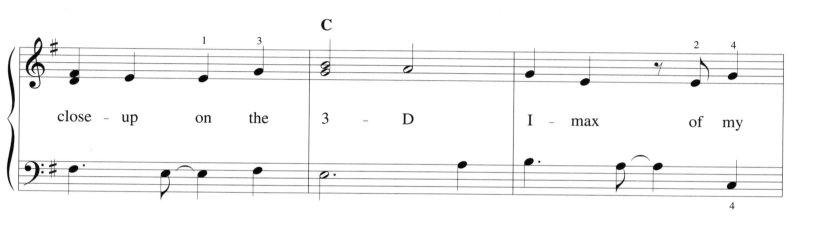

close - up on the 3 - D I - max of my

mind? *Spoken: That's poetic.* *That's*

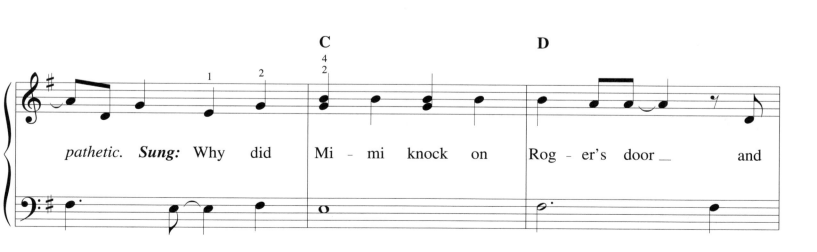

pathetic. **Sung:** Why did Mi - mi knock on Rog - er's door _ and

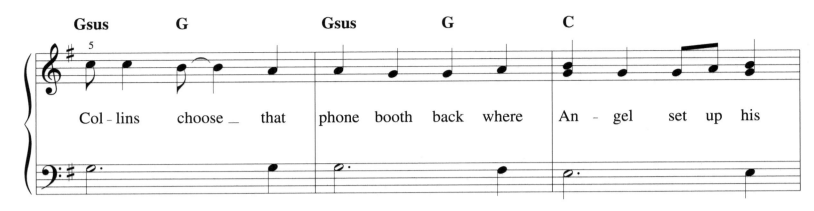

Col - lins   choose __ that   phone booth back where   An - gel   set up his

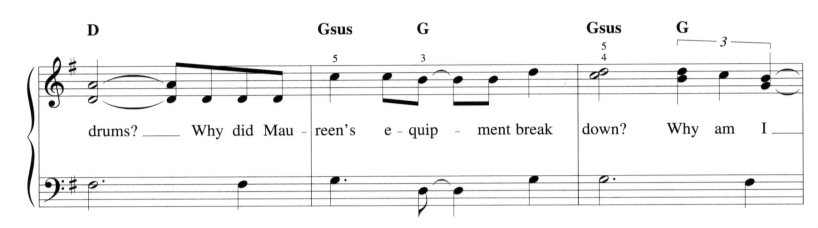

drums? _____ Why did Mau - reen's   e - quip - ment break   down?   Why am I __

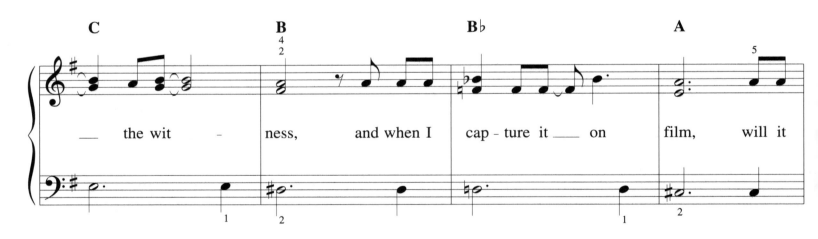

__ the wit - ness,   and when I   cap - ture it __ on   film,   will it

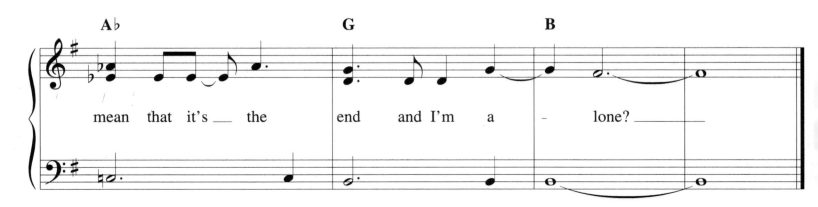

mean that it's __ the   end   and I'm a - lone? _____

I'LL COVER YOU

Words and Music by
JONATHAN LARSON

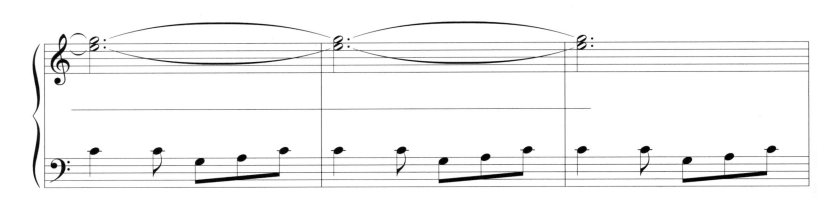

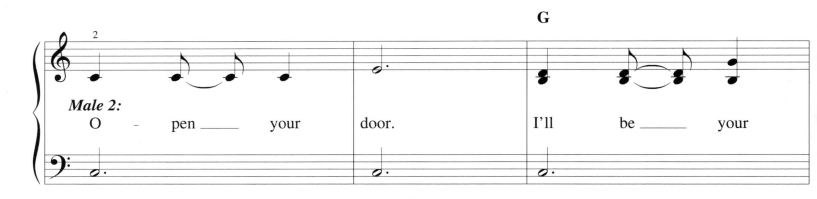

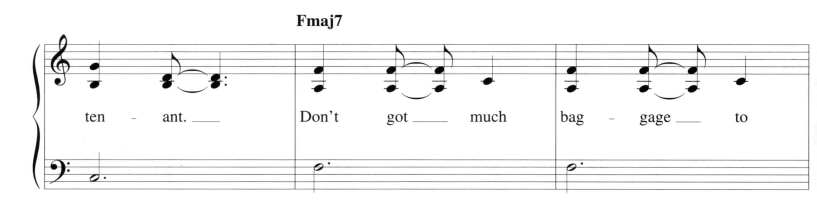

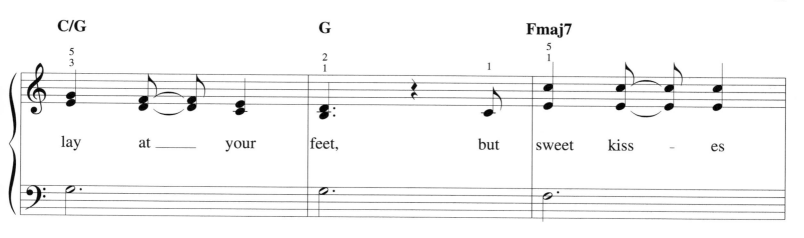

lay   at ___ your   feet,   but   sweet   kiss - es

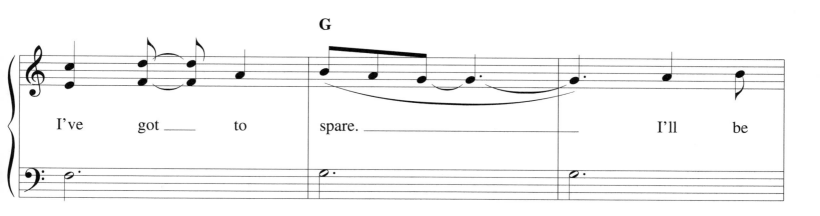

I've   got ___ to   spare. _____   I'll   be

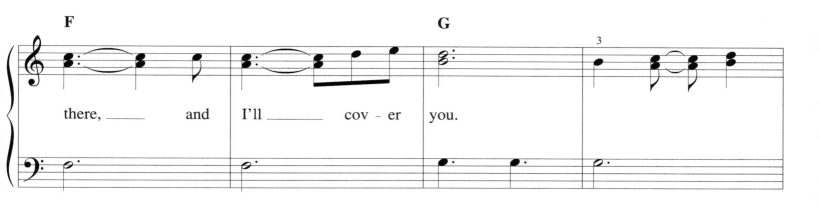

there, ___   and   I'll _____ cov - er   you.

Both:
I   think ___ they   meant   it ___ when they   said   you ___ can't

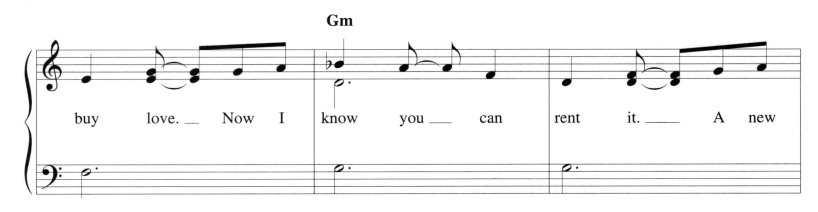

Gm

buy   love.   Now   I   know   you   can   rent   it.   A   new

E♭maj7   **A♭**

lease   you   are,   my   love,   on   life.

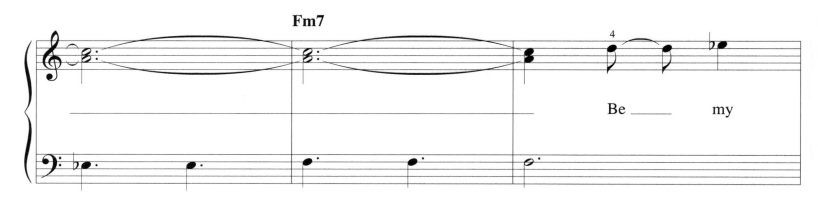

Fm7

Be   my

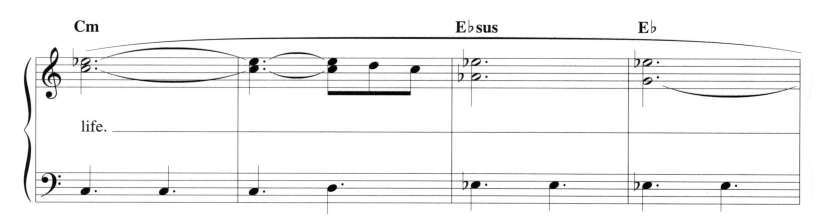

Cm   **E♭sus**   **E♭**

life.

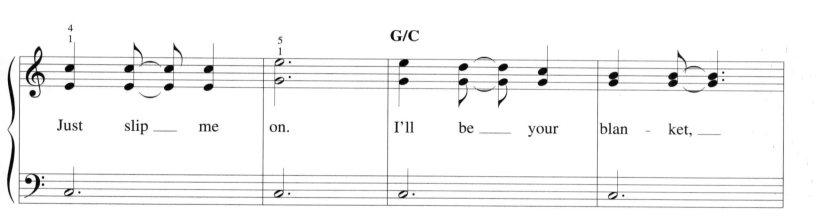

Just slip ___ me on. I'll be ___ your blan - ket, ___

wher - ev - er, what - ev - er. I'll be ___ your

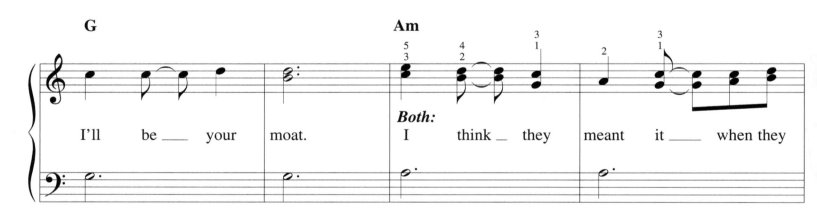

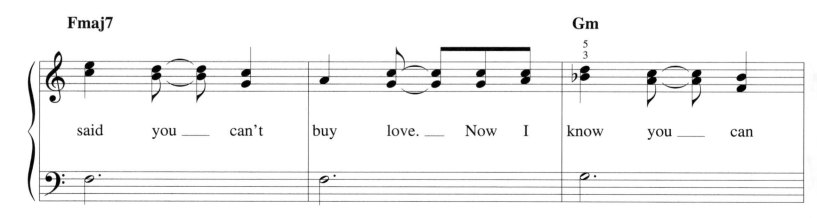

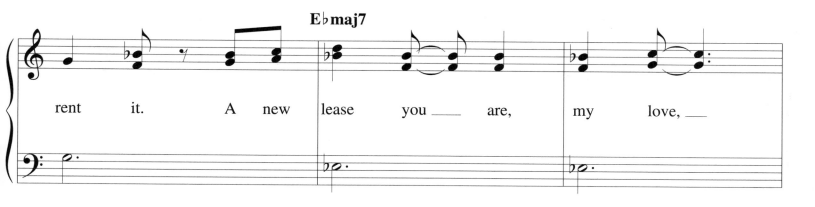

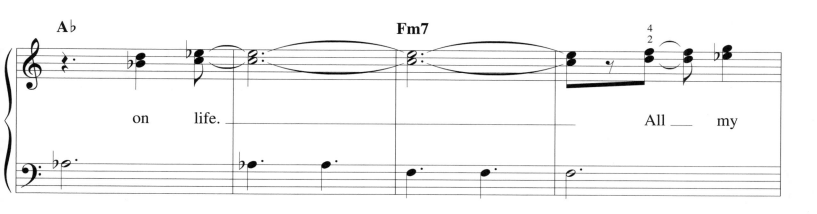

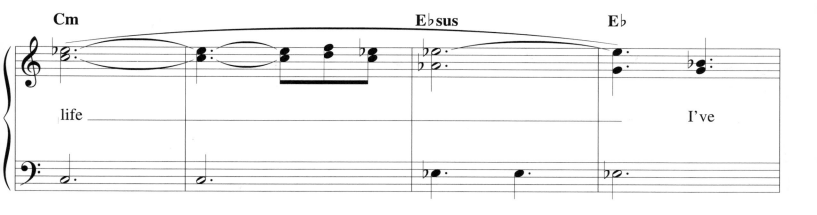

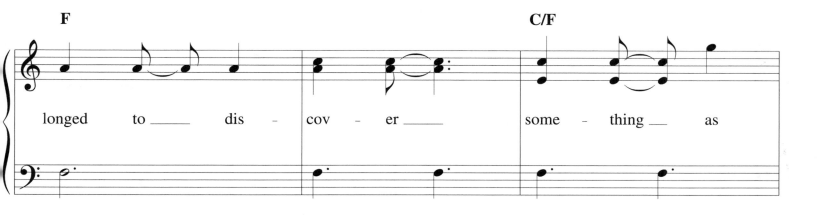

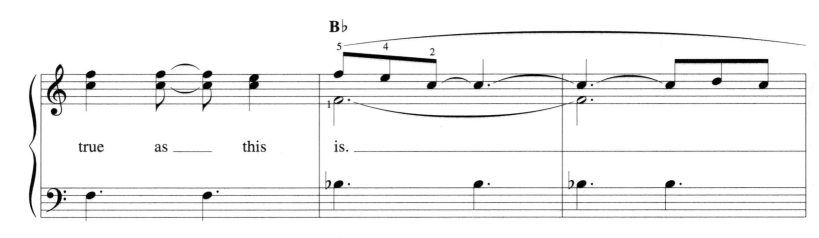

true as ___ this is. ___

Male 2:
So ___ with a thou - sand ___ sweet

kiss - es, if you're cold and ___ you're lone - ly, ___

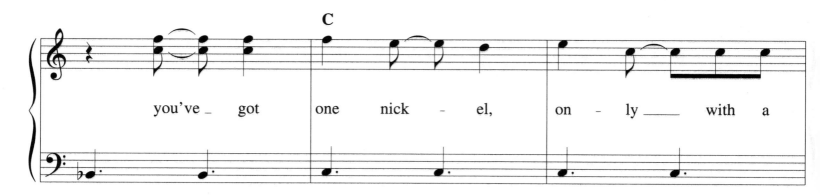

you've ___ got one nick - el, on - ly ___ with a

thou - sand __ sweet kiss - es. __ I'll

cov - er you __ with a thou - sand __ sweet kiss - es. __

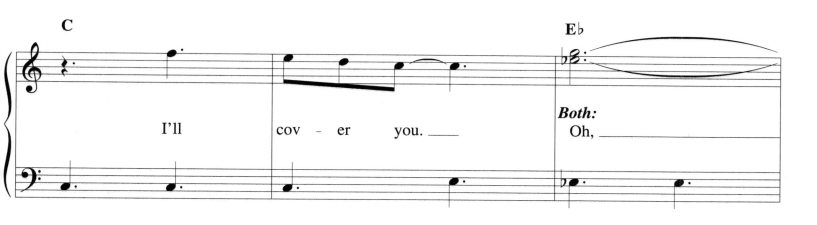

I'll cov - er you. __ *Both:* Oh, _____

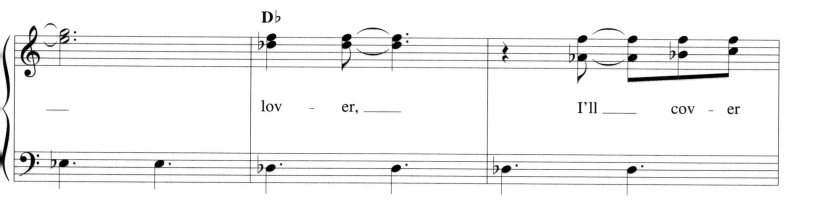

__ lov - er, __ I'll __ cov - er

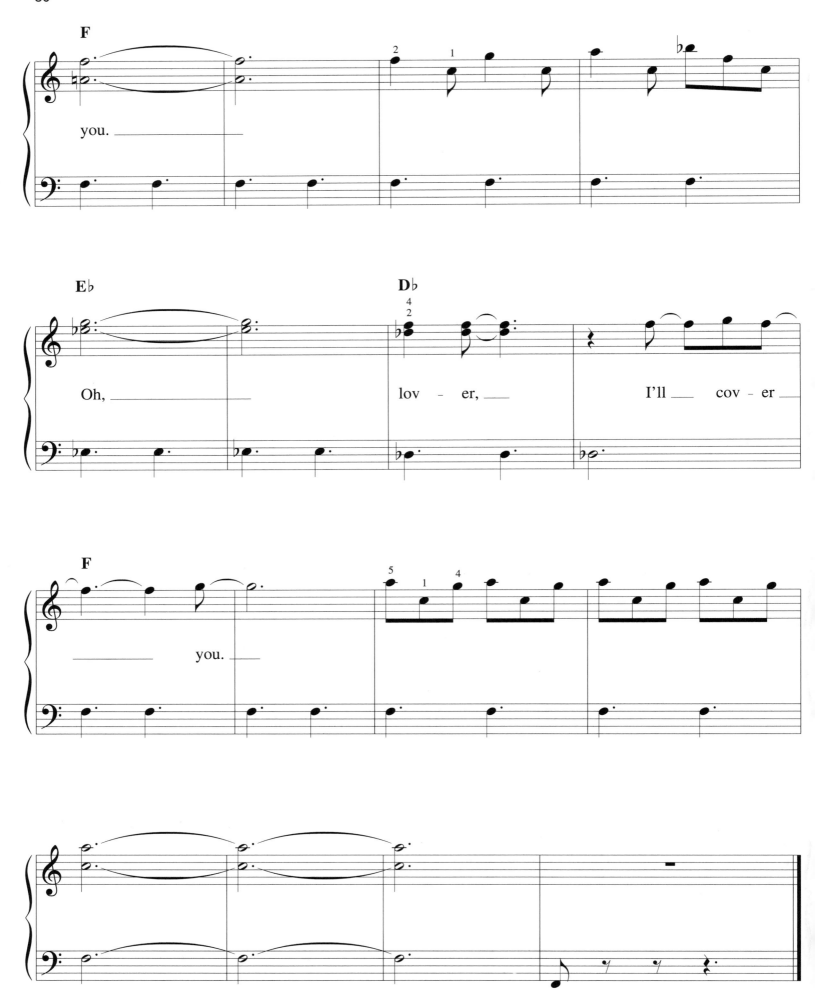

SANTA FE

Words and Music by
JONATHAN LARSON

Moderately

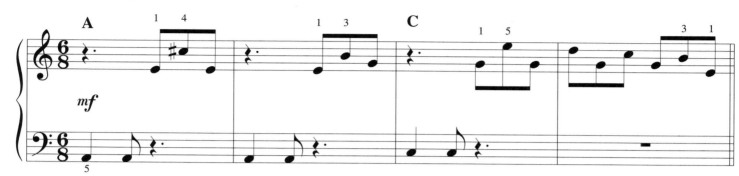

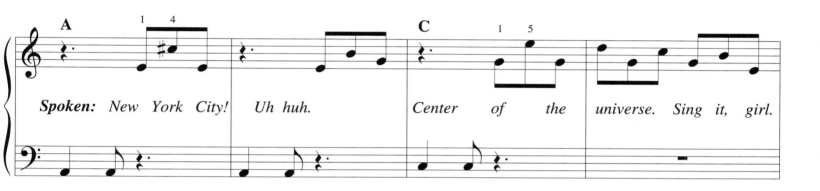

Spoken: New York City! Uh huh. Center of the universe. Sing it, girl.

Times are shitty, but I'm pretty sure they can't get worse. I hear ya.

It's a comfort to know when you're singing the "Hit the Road

Blues"　　　***Sung:*** that　an – y – where else you can　pos – si – bly go af – ter

New York __ would　be _____　　a pleas-ure cruise. __

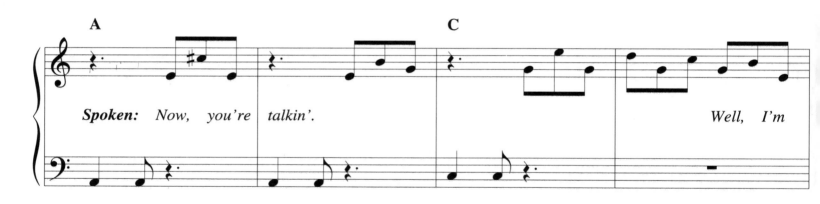

Spoken: *Now, you're talkin'.*　　　*Well, I'm*

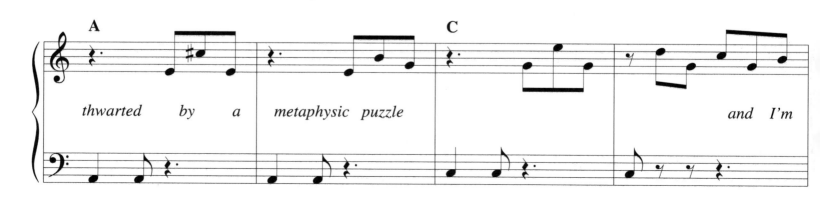

thwarted　by　a　metaphysic puzzle　　　and I'm

A   **C**

sick of grading   *papers, that I know.*   ***Sung:***   I'm

A   **C**

shout - ing in my   sleep; I ___ need a   muz - zle.

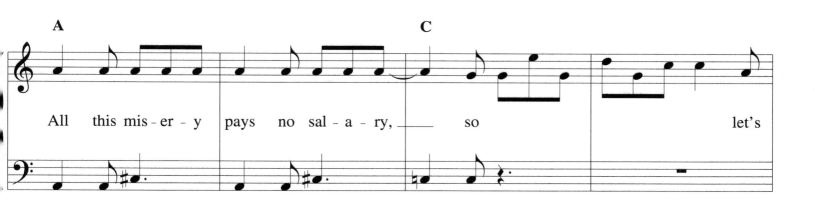

A   **C**

All this mis - er - y   pays no sal - a - ry, ___ so   let's

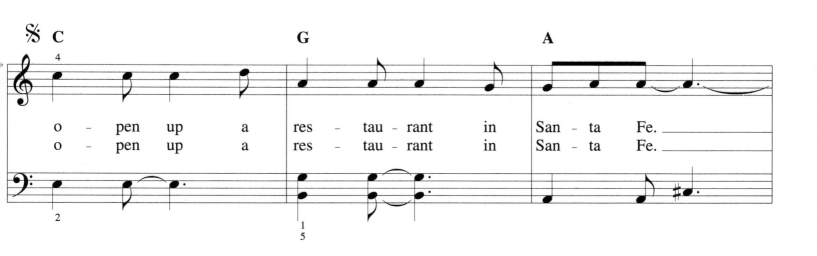

C   **G**   **A**

o - pen up   a   res - tau - rant   in   San - ta   Fe. ___

o - pen up   a   res - tau - rant   in   San - ta   Fe. ___

Our Sun-ny San-ta Fe ___ would be ___ nice.
Our la-bors would reap fi - nan - cial ___ gain.

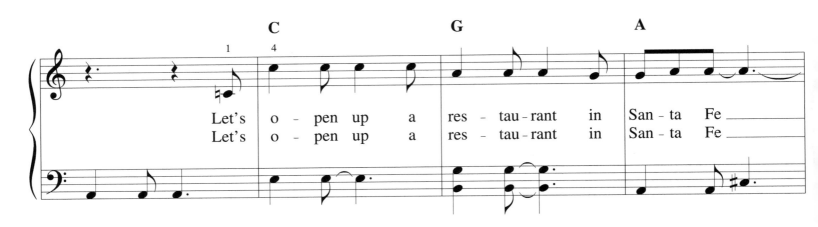

Let's o-pen up a res-tau-rant in San-ta Fe ___
Let's o-pen up a res-tau-rant in San-ta Fe ___

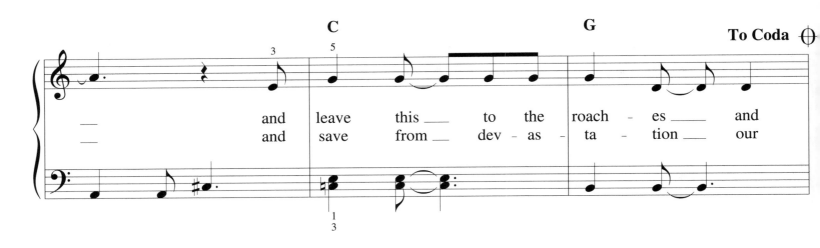

To Coda

___ and leave this ___ to the roach - es ___ and
___ and save from ___ dev-as - ta - tion ___ our

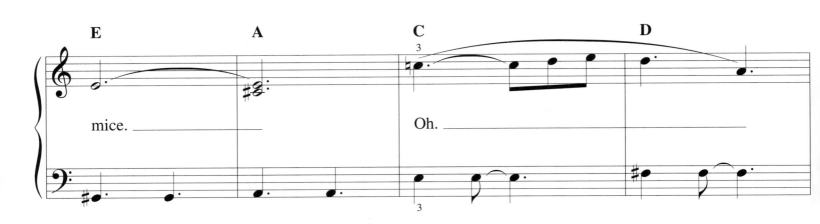

mice. ___ Oh. ___

55

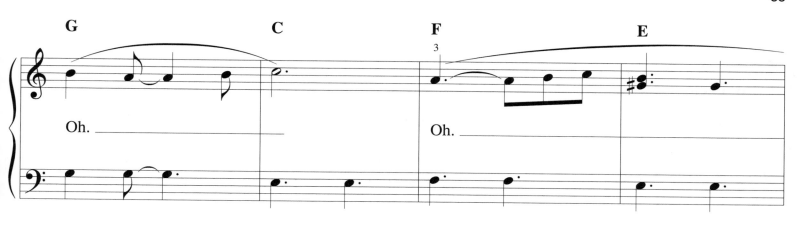

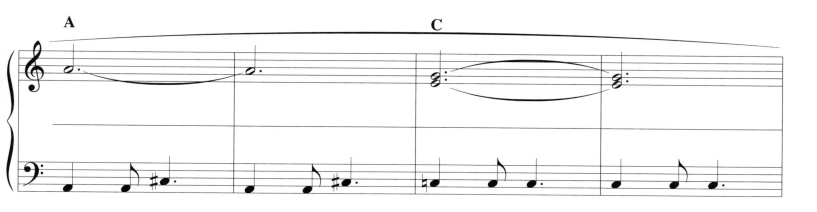

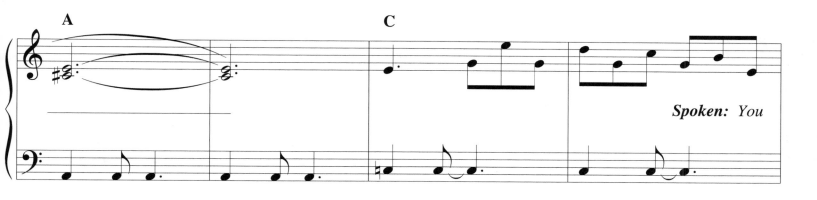

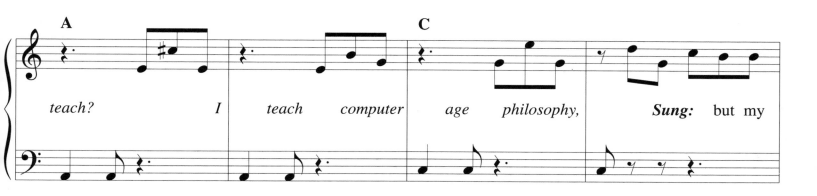

stu-dents would rath-er watch___ T. V. *Spoken:* *Huh, America,* *America,* *Sung:* You're a

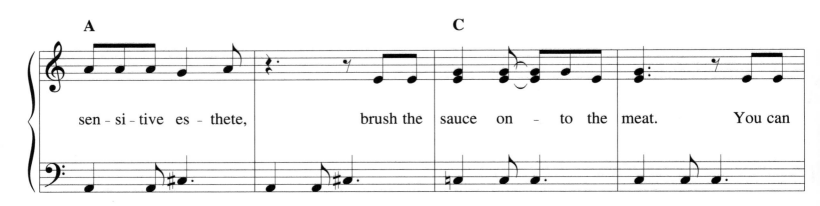

sen - si - tive es - thete, brush the sauce on - to the meat. You can

make the men - u spar - kle ___ with ___ rhyme. _____ *Spoken:* *You could*

drum a gentle beat, *And I could* *seat guests as they come,* *Sung:* chat-ting

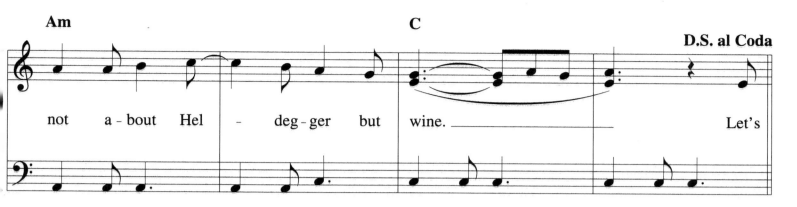

not a-bout Hel - deg-ger but wine. _____ Let's

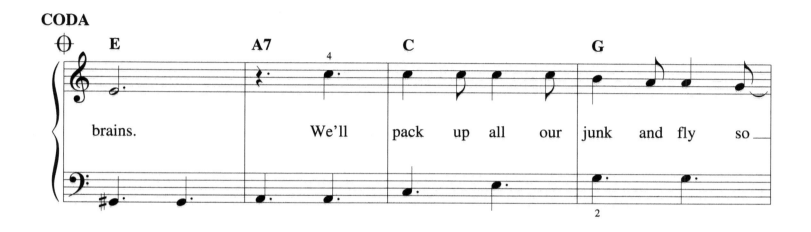

CODA

brains. We'll pack up all our junk and fly so___

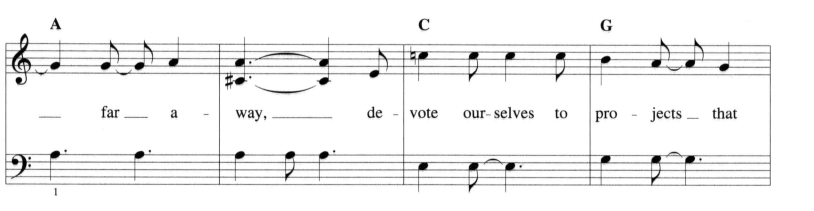

___ far a - way, _____ de-vote our-selves to pro - jects __ that

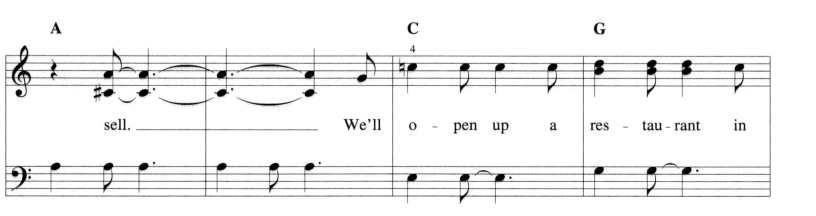

sell. _____ We'll o - pen up a res - tau - rant in

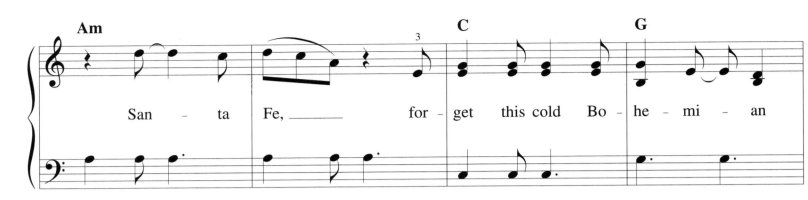

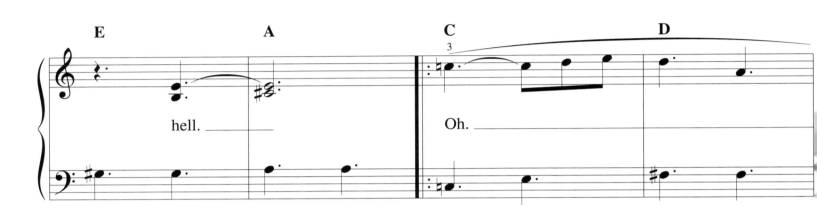

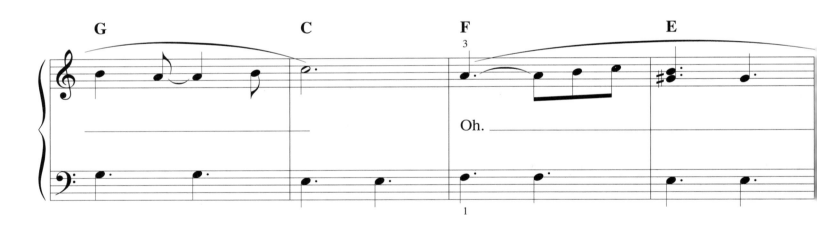

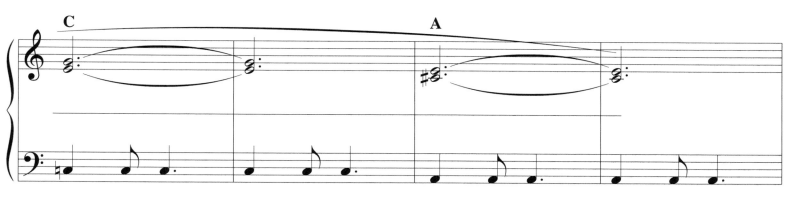

Do you know the

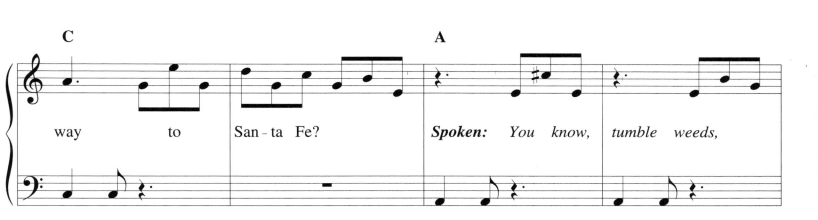

way to San-ta Fe? **Spoken:** *You know, tumble weeds,*

prairie dogs. *Yeah!*

ONE SONG GLORY

Words and Music by
JONATHAN LARSON

Moderately

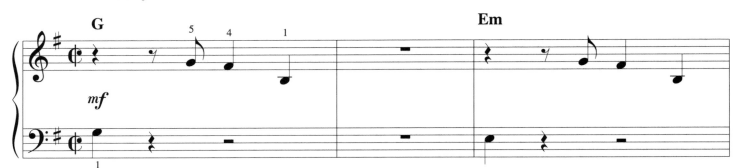

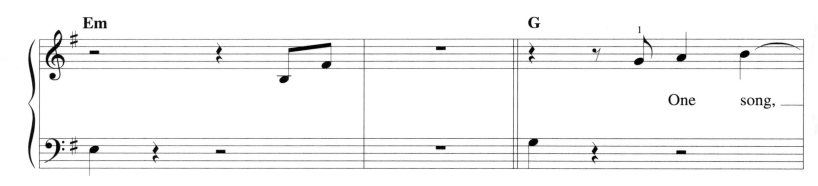

One song,

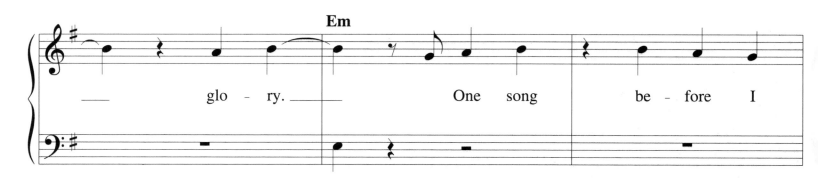

___ glo - ry. ___ One song be - fore I

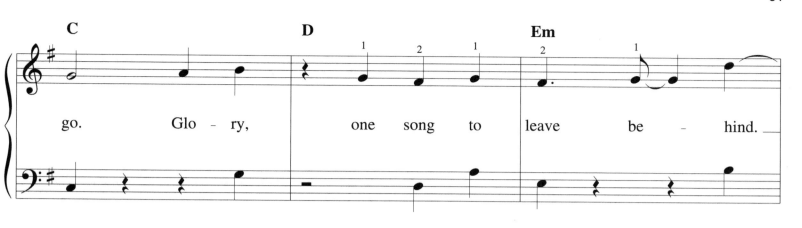

go. Glo - ry, one song to leave be - hind.

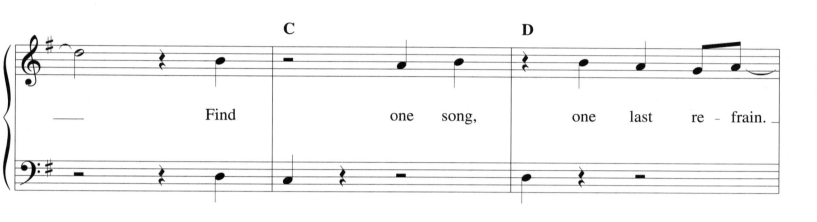

Find one song, one last re - frain.

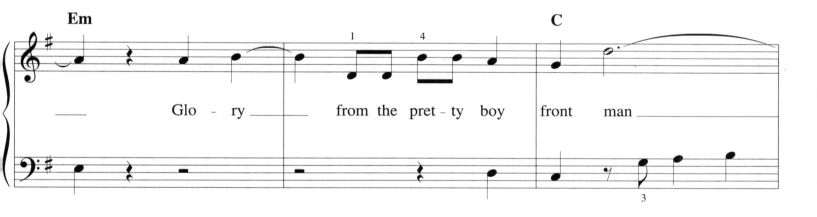

Glo - ry from the pret - ty boy front man

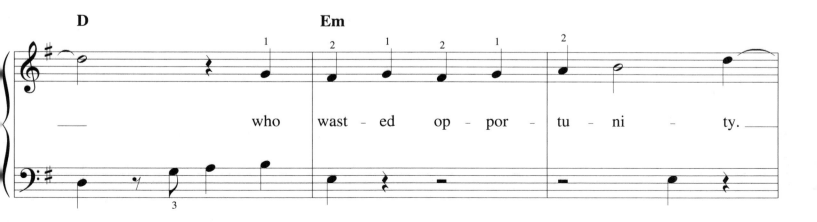

who wast - ed op - por - tu - ni - ty.

One song, he had the world at his feet. Glo - ry

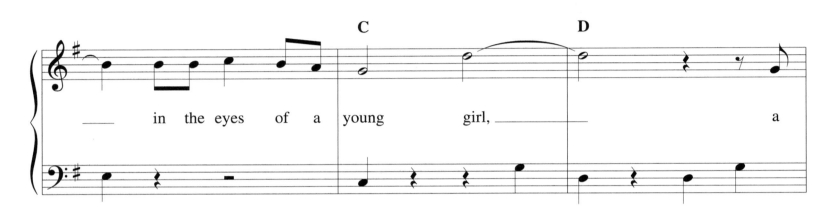

in the eyes of a young girl, a

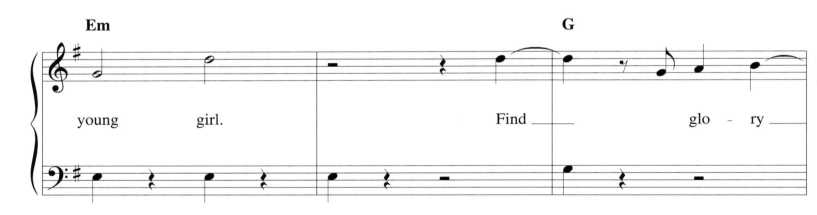

young girl. Find glo - ry

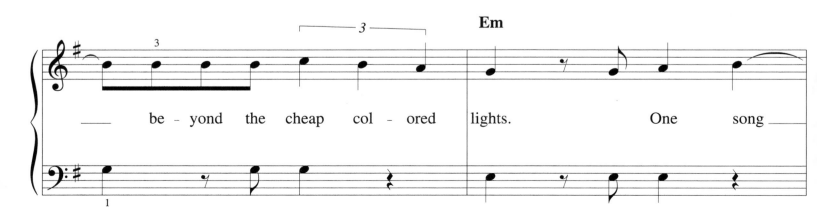

be - yond the cheap col - ored lights. One song

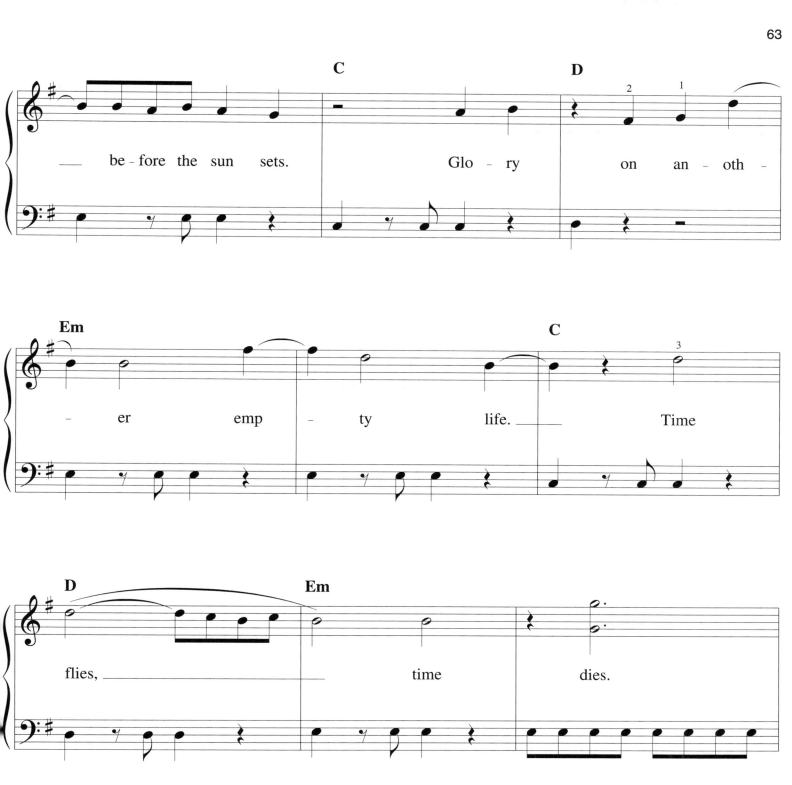

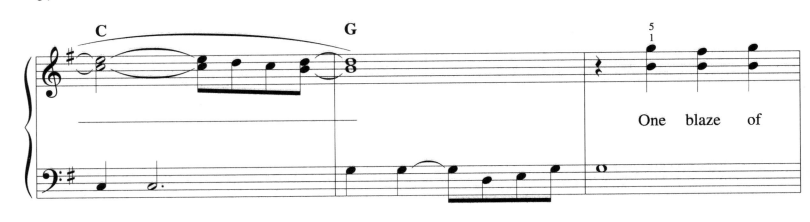

One blaze of

glo - ry. ____

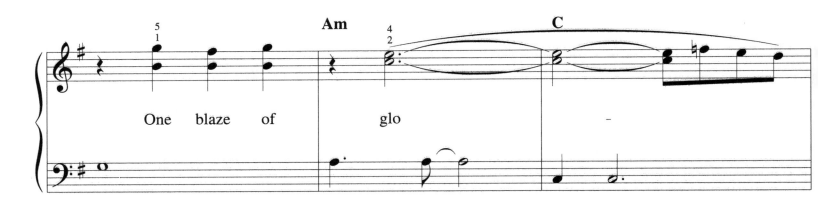

One blaze of glo -

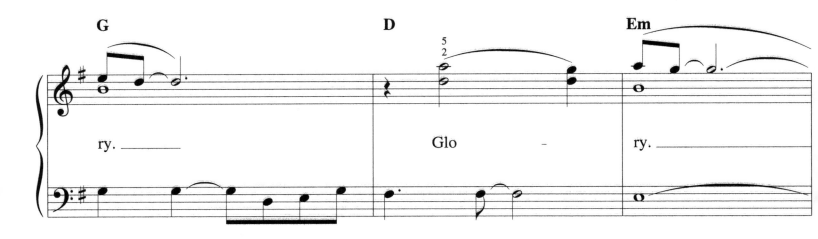

ry. ____ Glo - ry. ____

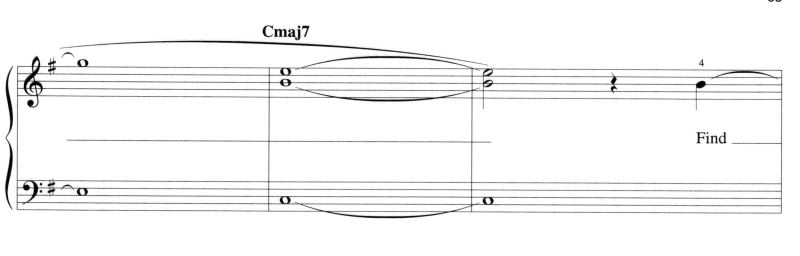

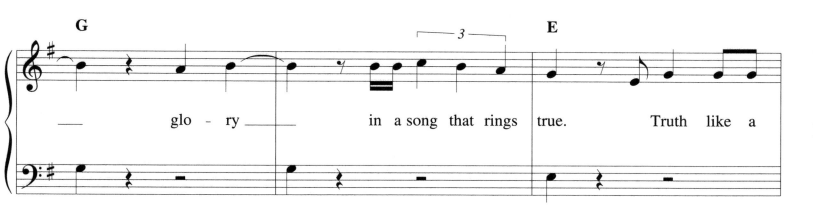

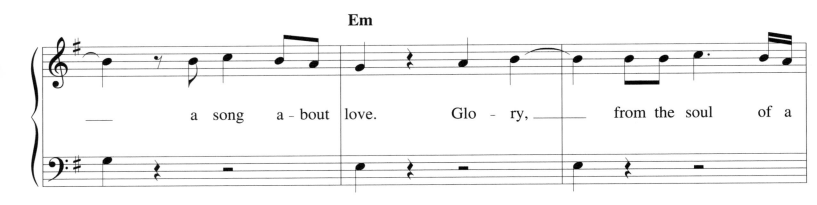

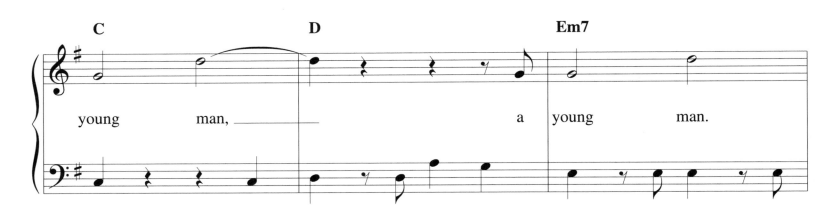

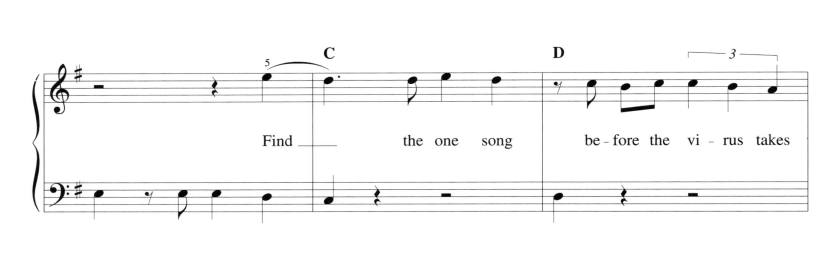

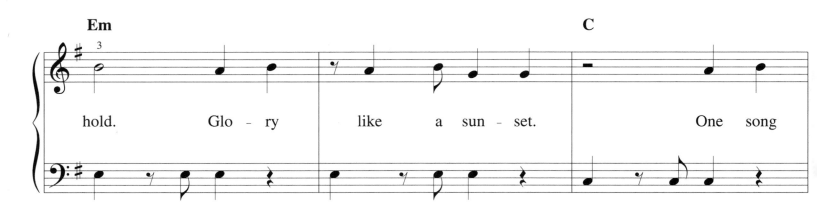

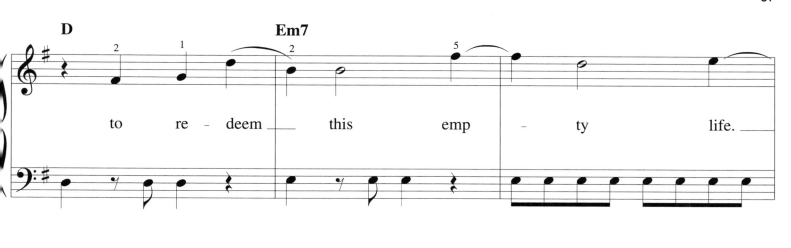

to re - deem this emp - ty life.

Time flies and then no need

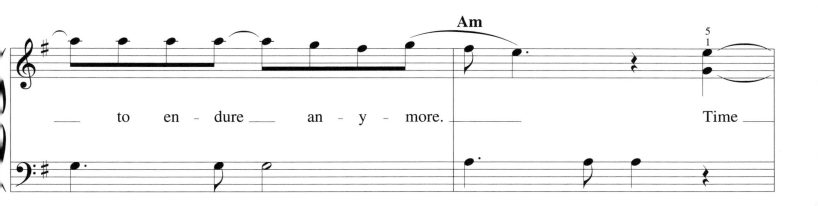

to en - dure an - y - more. Time

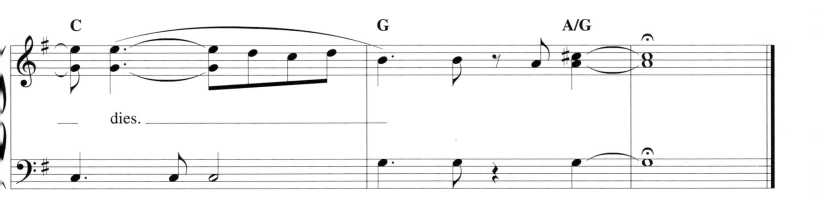

dies.

SEASONS OF LOVE

Words and Music by
JONATHAN LARSON

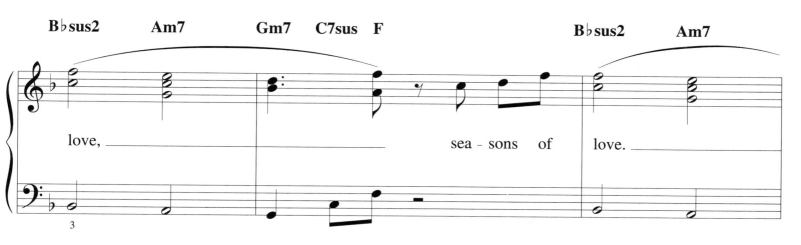

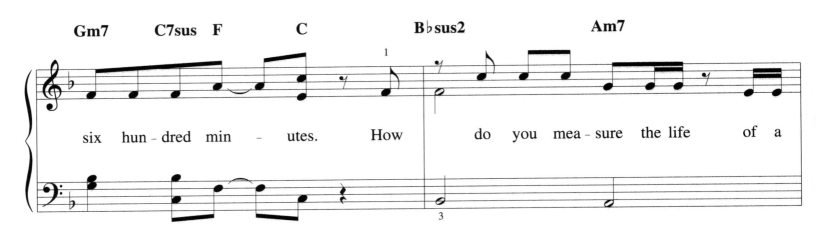

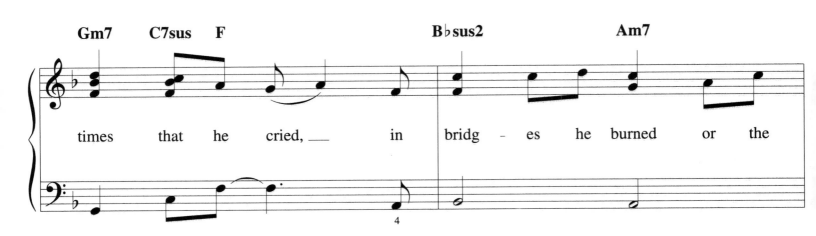

re - mem-ber the love,

mea - sure in love.

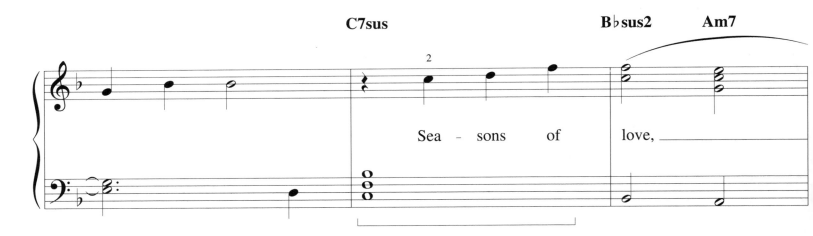

Sea - sons of love,

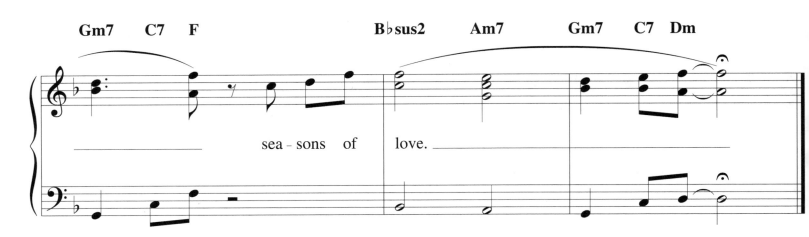

sea - sons of love.

ANOTHER DAY

Words and Music by
JONATHAN LARSON

Moderately bright

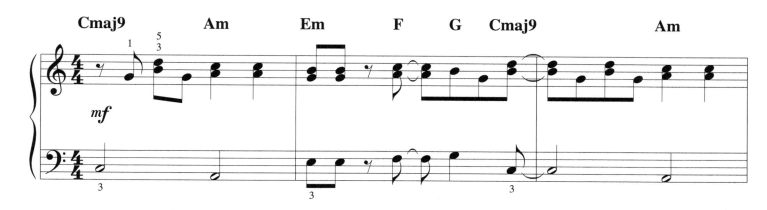

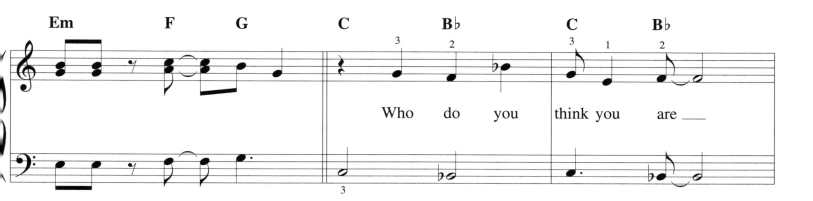

Who do you think you are ___

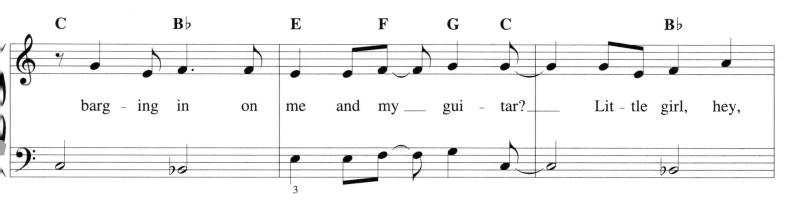

barg - ing in on me and my ___ gui - tar? ___ Lit - tle girl, hey,

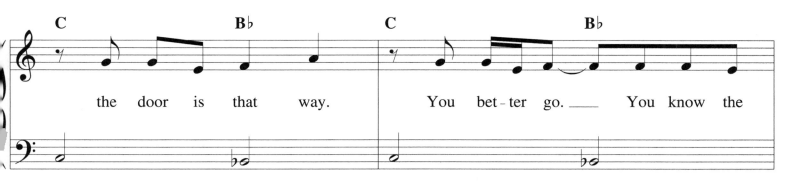

the door is that way. You bet - ter go. ___ You know the

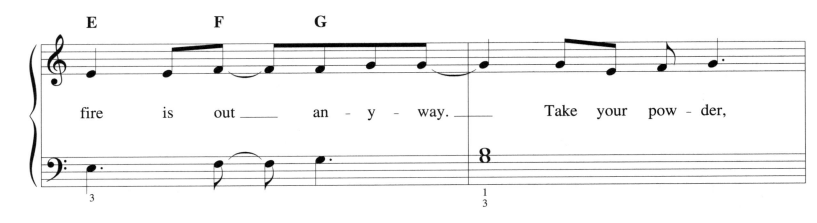

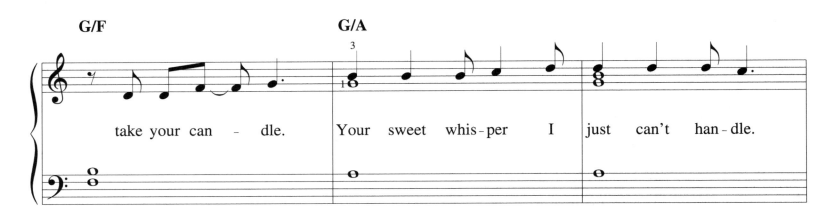

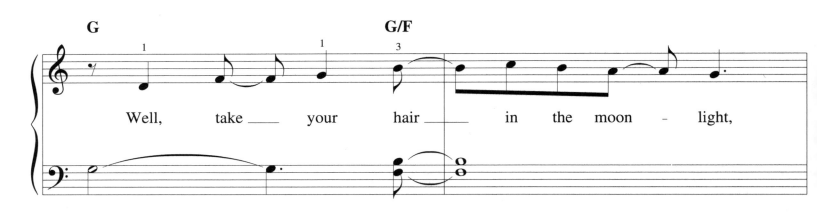

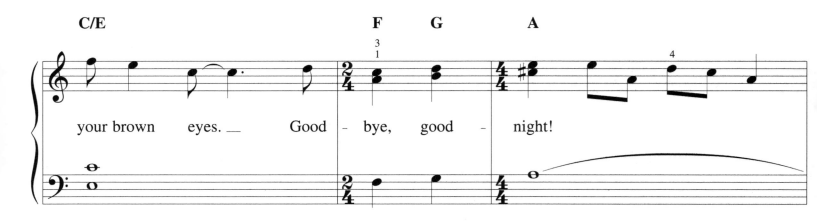

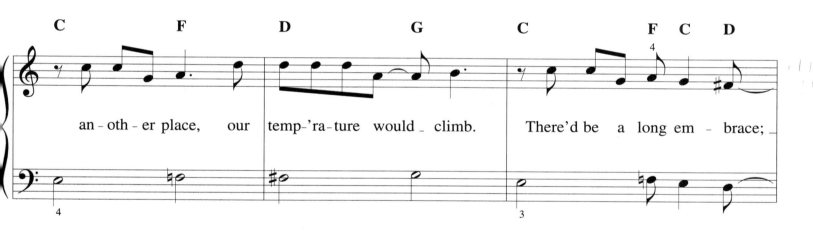

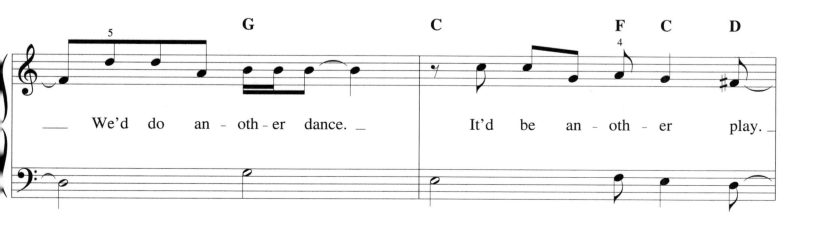

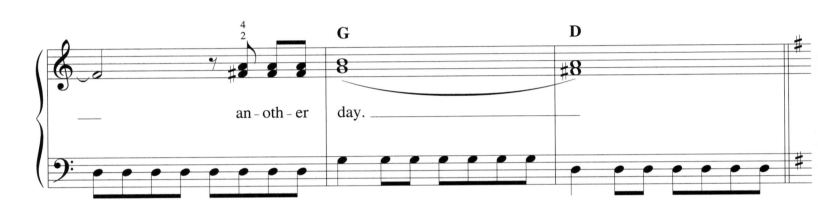

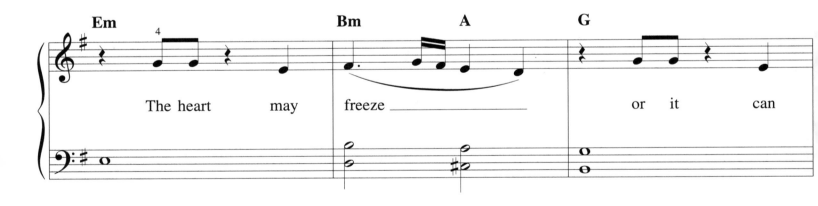

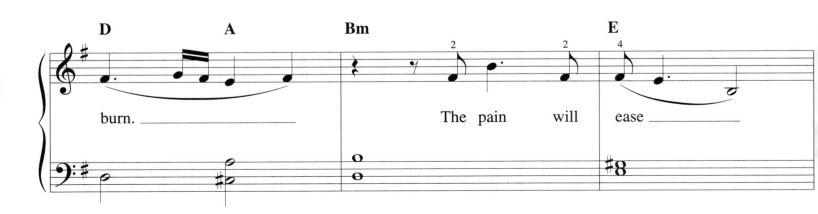

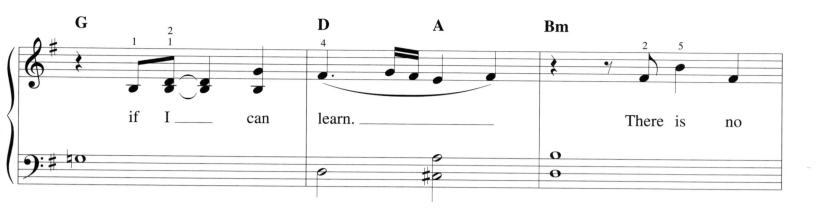

if I ____ can learn. _____ There is no

fu - ture. _____ There is no past. _____

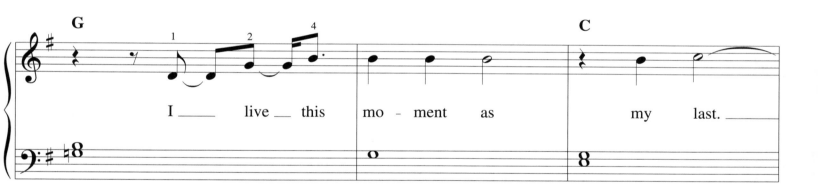

I ____ live ____ this mo - ment as my last. _____

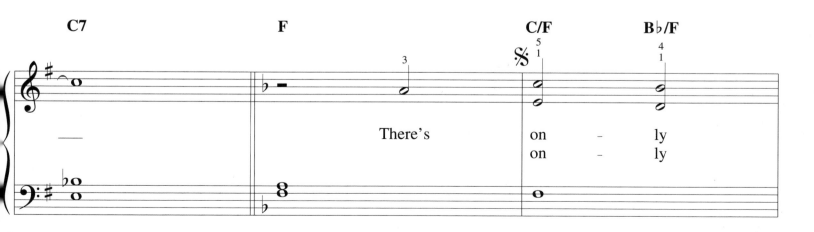

____ There's on - ly
on - ly

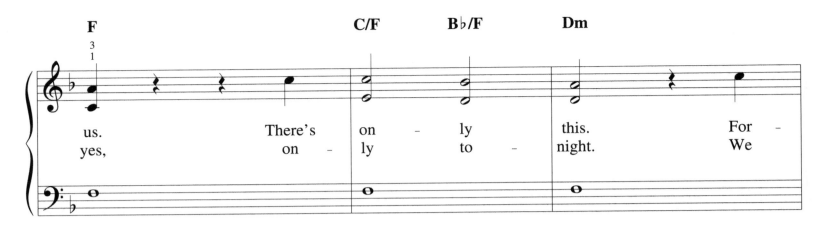

us. / yes, There's on - ly / on - ly to - this. / night. For - / We

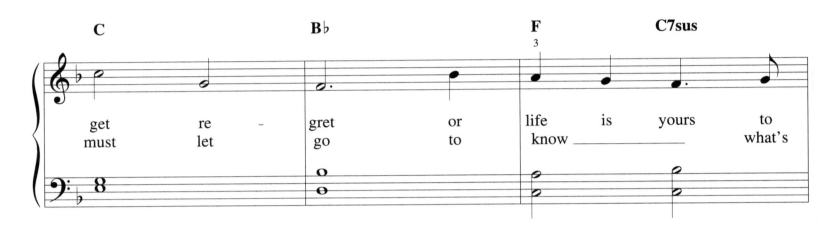

get re - / must let gret / go or / to life is yours to / know _____ what's

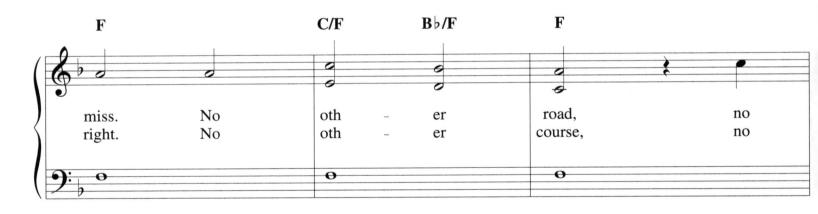

miss. / right. No oth - er / No oth - er road, / course, no / no

oth - er _____ way, _____ no day but to - day. / oth - er _____ way, _____ no day but to - day.

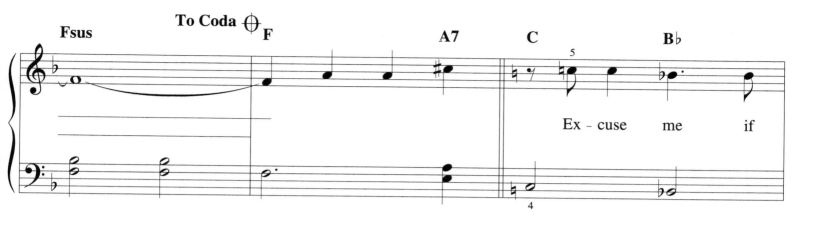

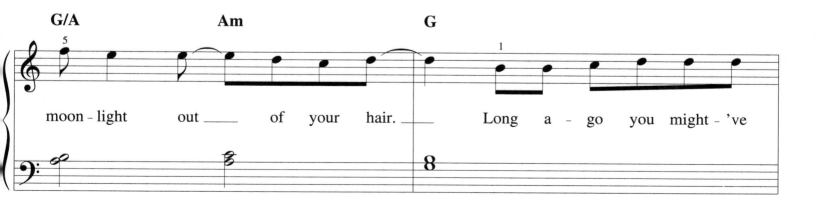

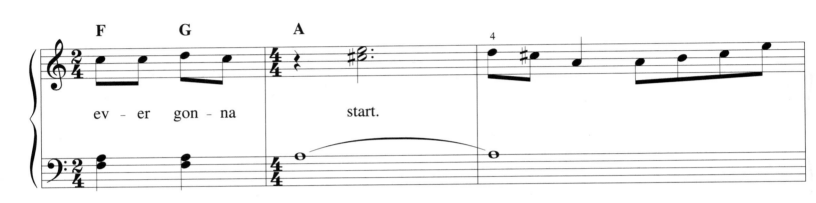

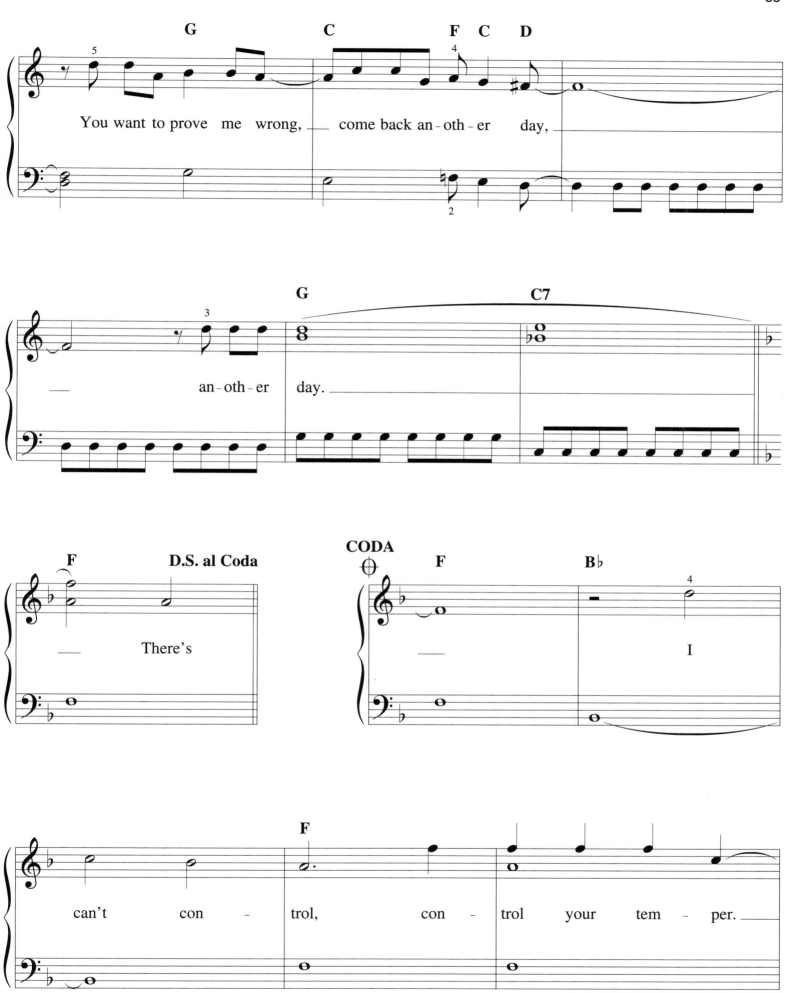

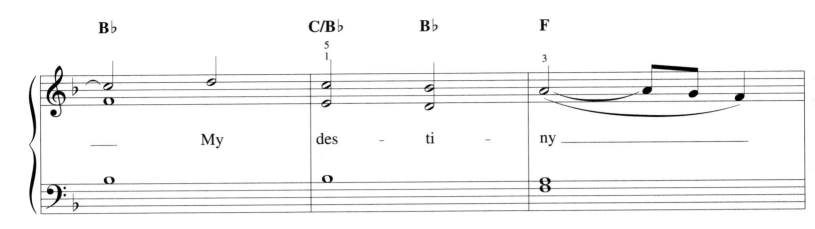

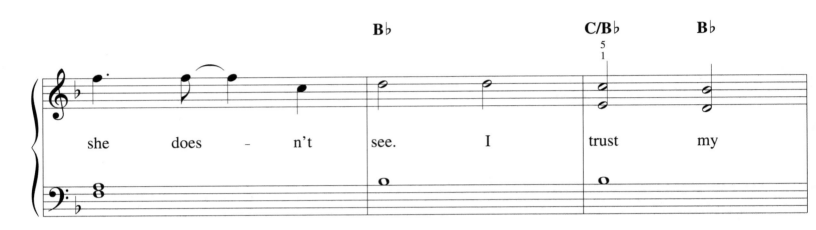

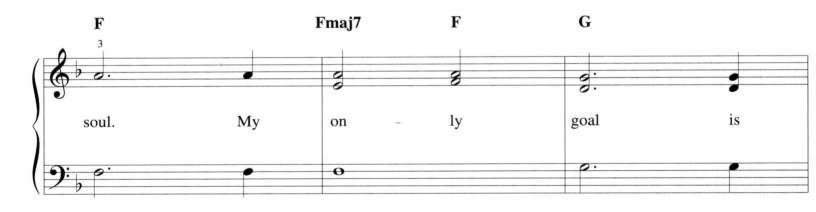

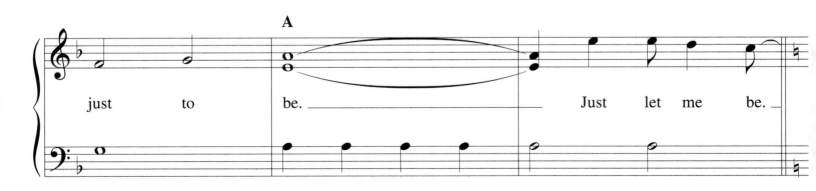

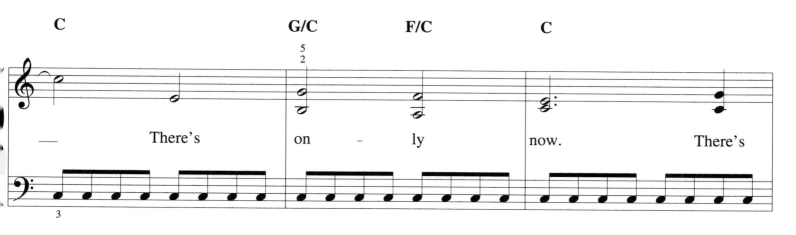

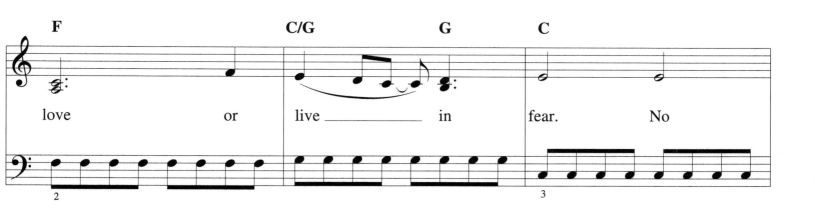

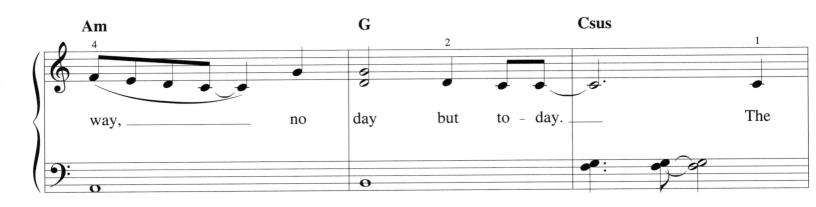

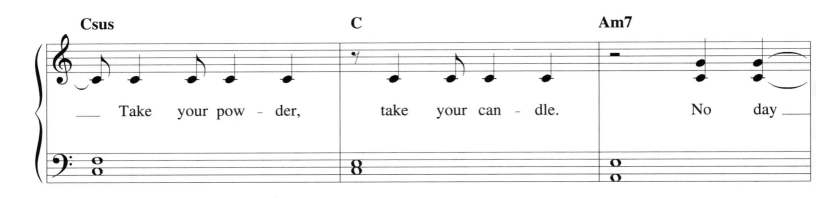

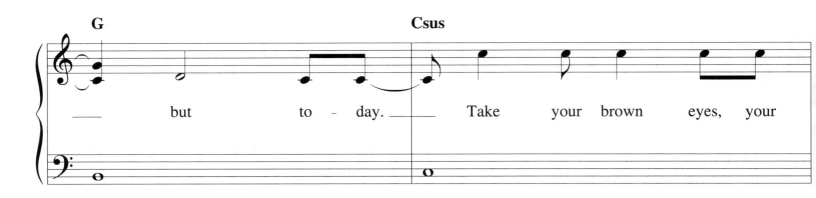

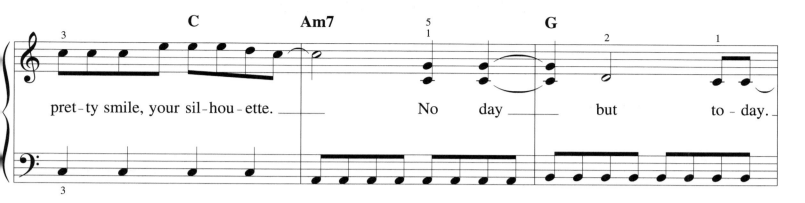

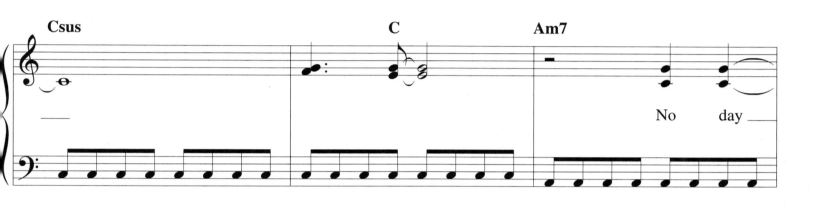

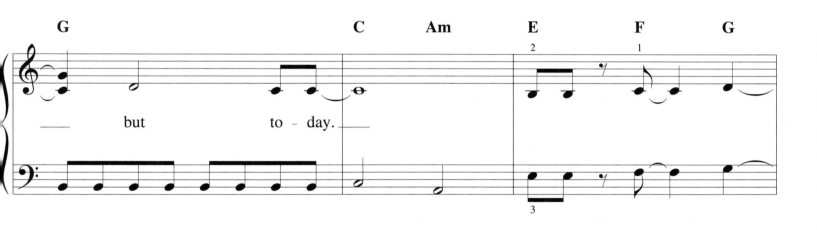

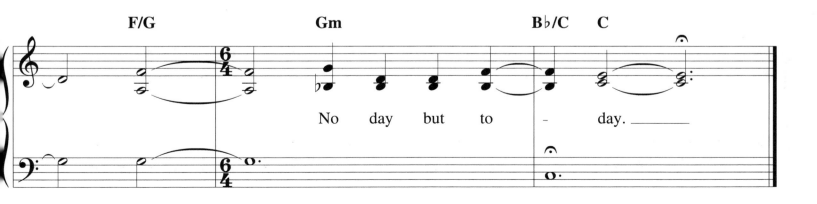

WHAT YOU OWN

Words and Music by
JONATHAN LARSON

Medium Rock

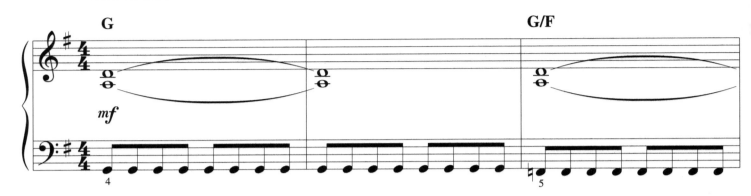

Don't breathe too deep.

Don't think all day. Dive in-to work.

Drive the oth-er way.

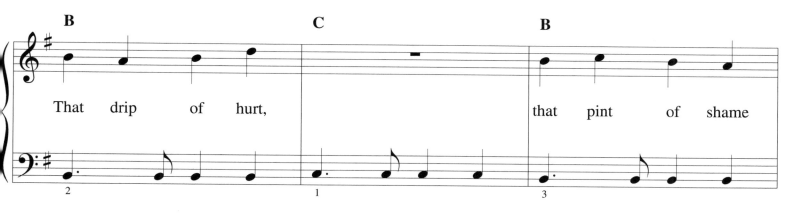

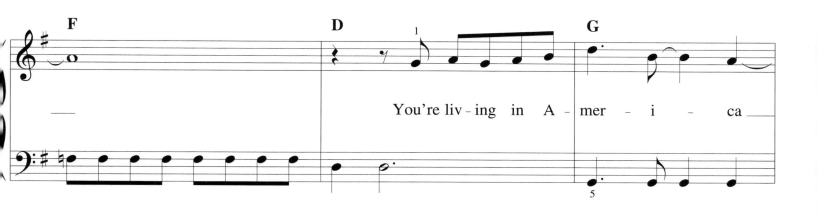

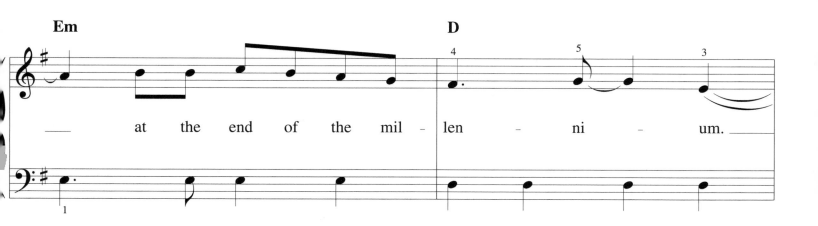

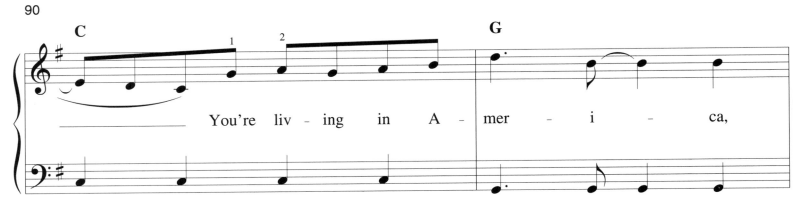

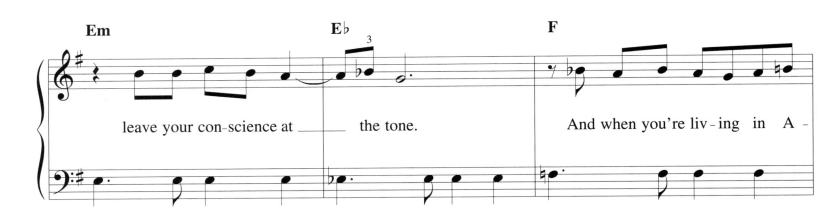

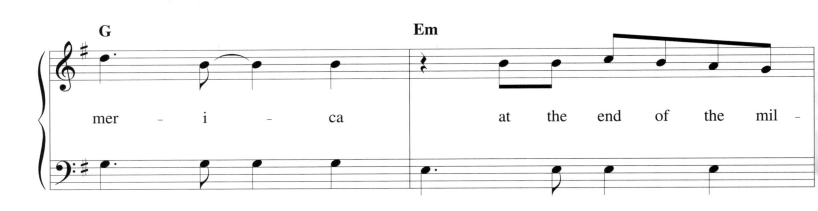

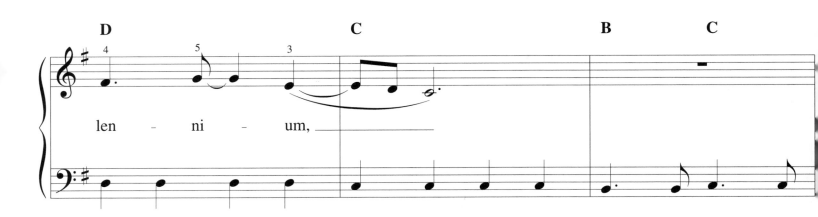

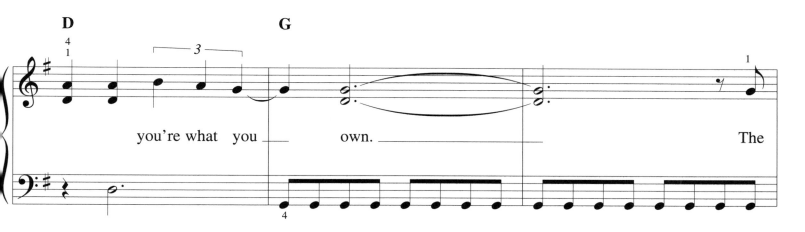

you're what you own. The

film - mak-er can-not see, and the song - writ-er can-not hear.

Yet I see Mi - mi ev - 'ry - where. An-gel's

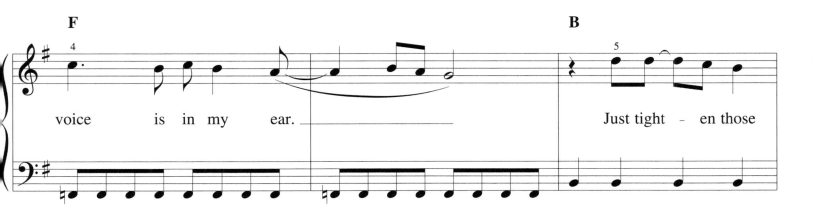

voice is in my ear. Just tight - en those

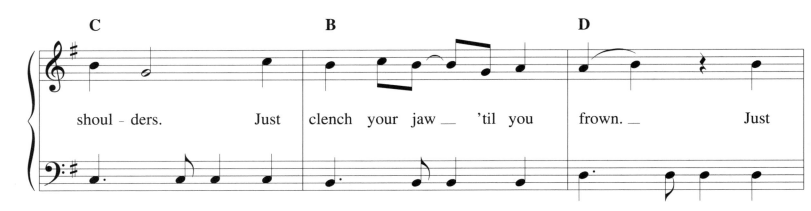

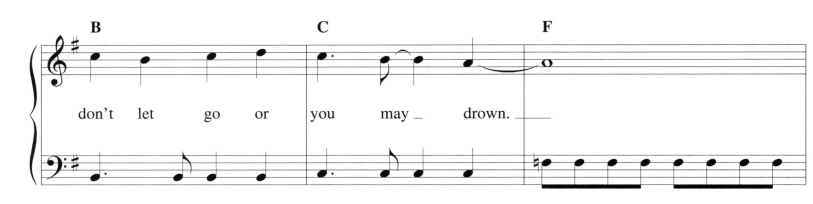

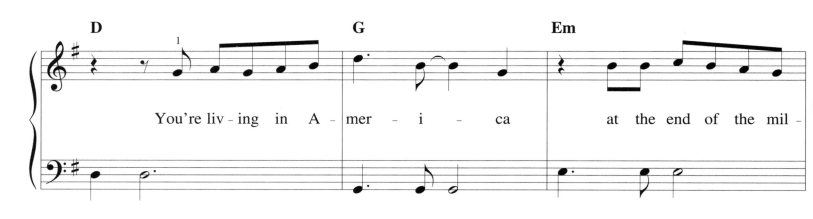

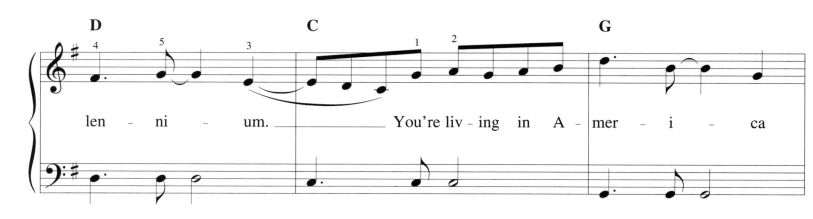

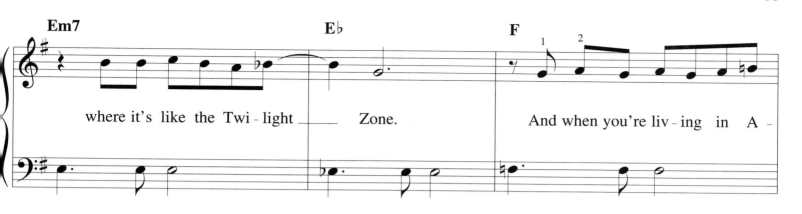

where it's like the Twi-light Zone. And when you're liv-ing in A-

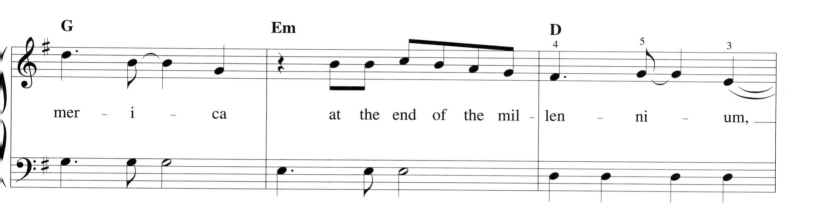

mer - i - ca at the end of the mil - len - ni - um,

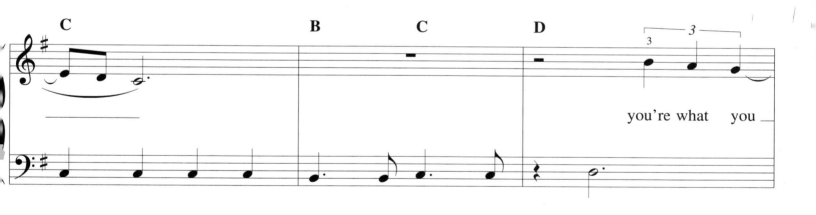

you're what you

own. So I own not a no-

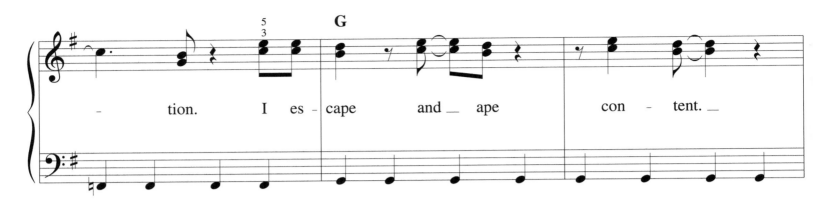

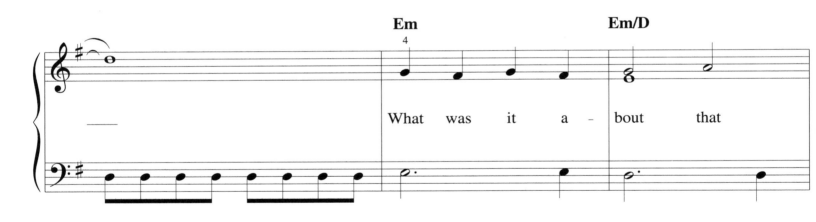

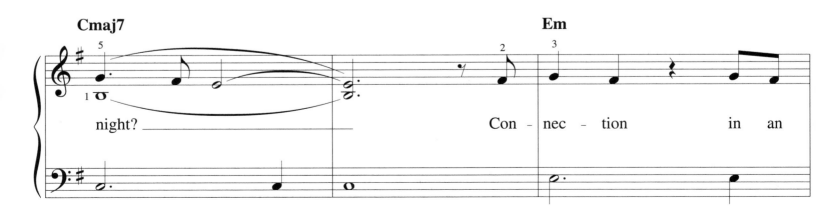

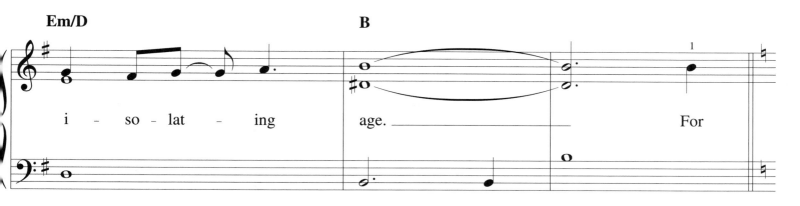

i - so - lat - ing age. _____ For

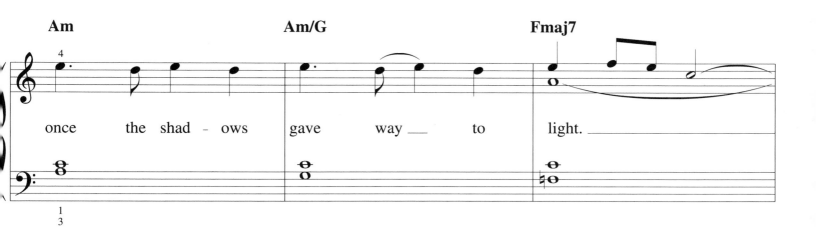

once the shad - ows gave way ___ to light. _____

_____ For once I did - n't dis - en - gage.

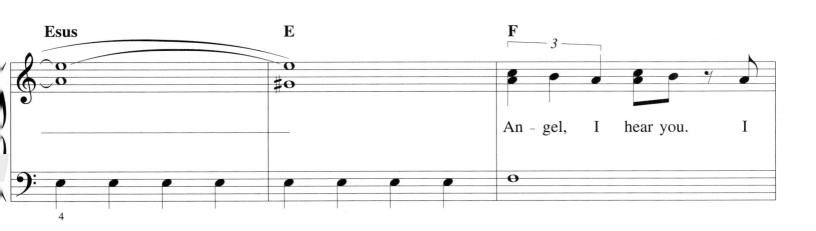

An - gel, I hear you. I

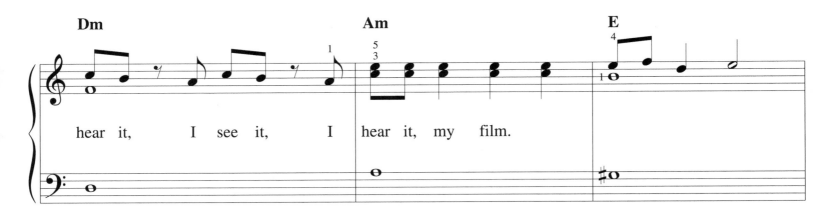

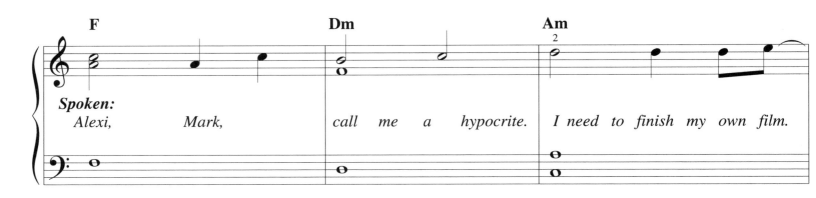

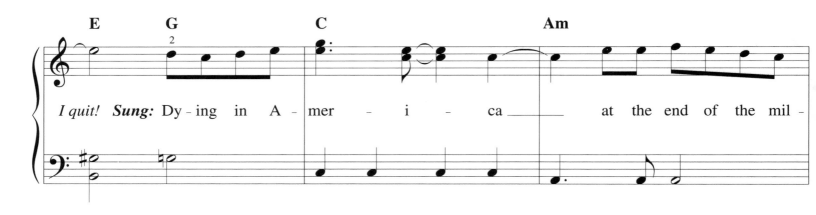

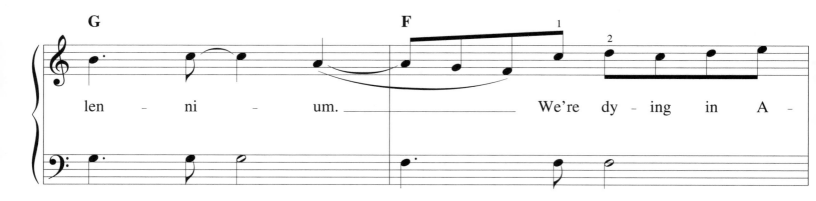

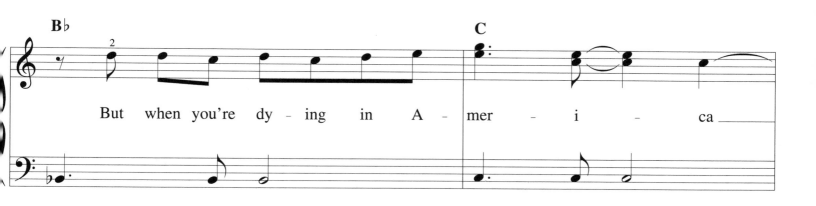

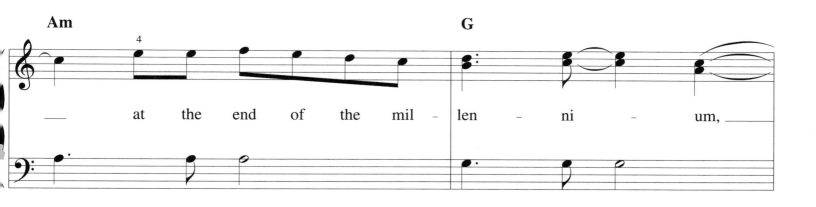

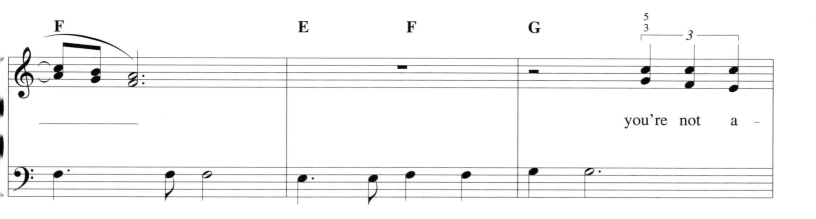

lone.

I'm not a - lone.

I'm not a - lone.

TAKE ME OR LEAVE ME

Words and Music by
JONATHAN LARSON

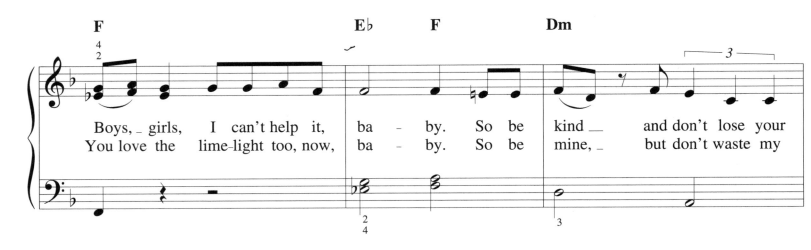

Boys, _ girls, I can't help it, ba - by. So be kind _ and don't lose your
You love the lime-light too, now, ba - by. So be mine, _ but don't waste my

mind. _____ Just re - mem - ber that I'm your
time. _____ Cry - in', "Oh, my honey bear, are you still my

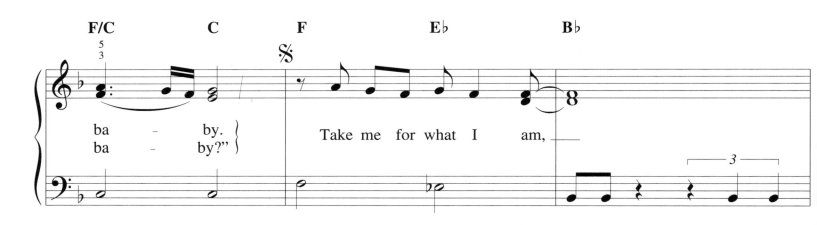

ba - by.
ba - by?"

Take me for what I am, _

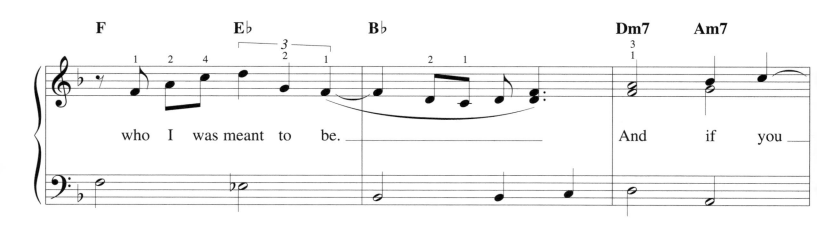

who I was meant to be. _____ And if you

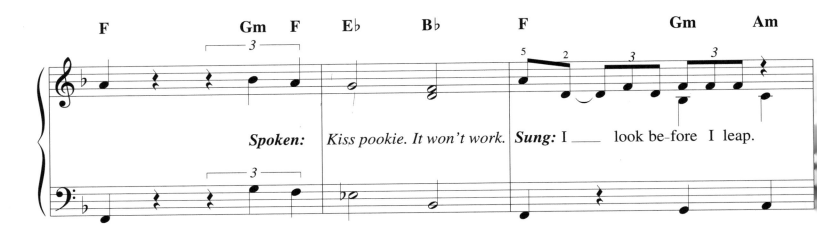

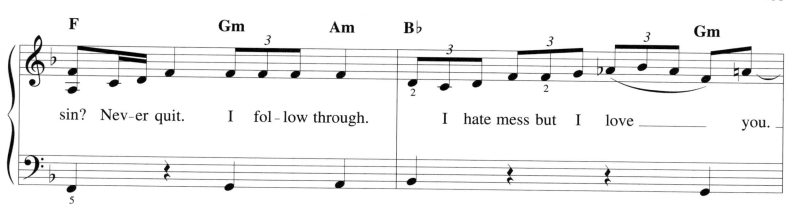

sin? Nev-er quit. I fol-low through. I hate mess but I love _____ you.

___ What to do with my im-promp-tu, ba - by?___ So be wise, __ 'cause this girl _ sat-is-

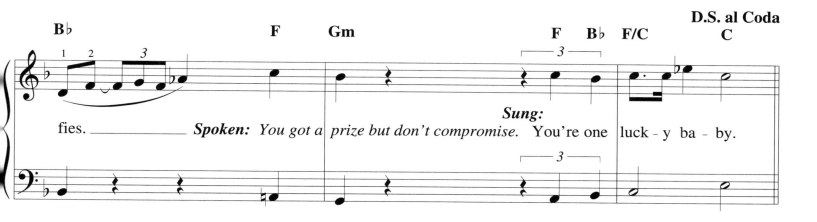

fies. _____ **Spoken:** *You got a prize but don't compromise.* You're one luck-y ba - by.

D.S. al Coda

Sung:

CODA

or leave me. That's it, ___ the straw that breaks my back.

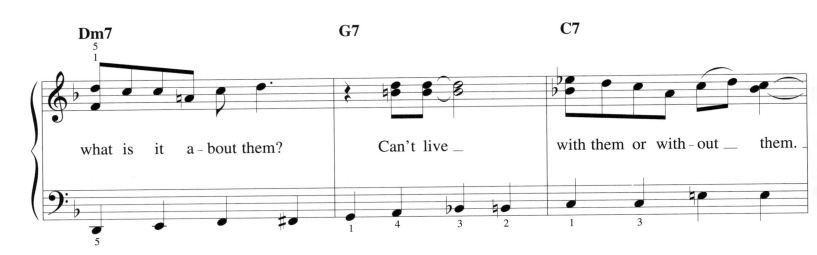

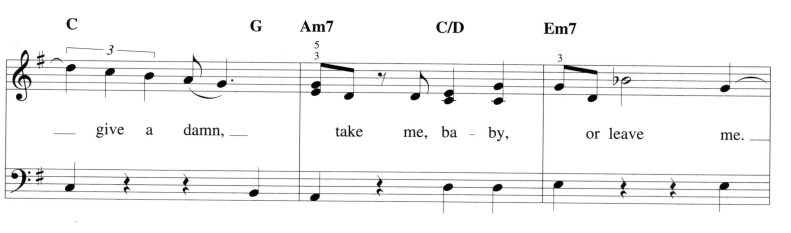

YOUR EYES

Words and Music by
JONATHAN LARSON

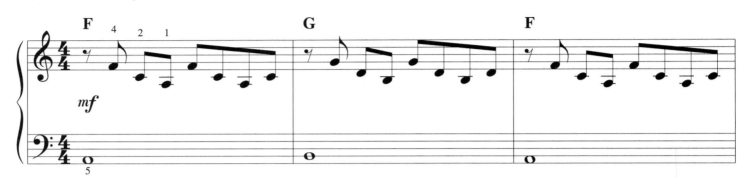

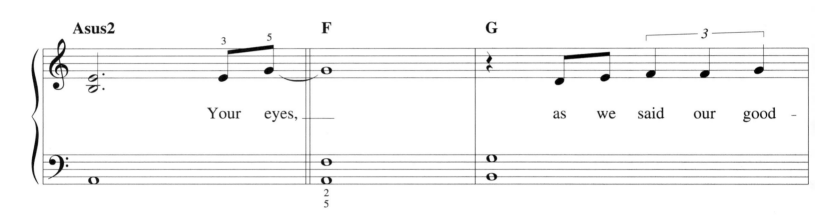

Your eyes,   as we said our good-

byes,   can't get them out of my mind.   And I

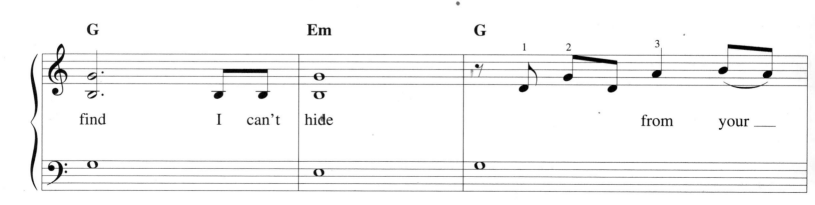

find   I can't hide   from your ___

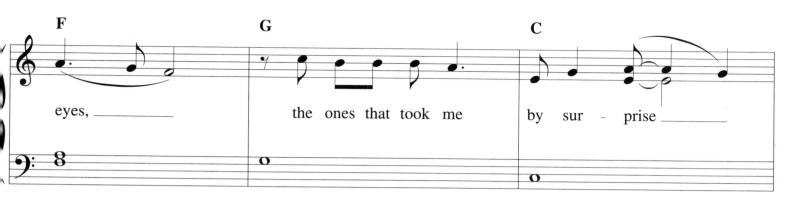

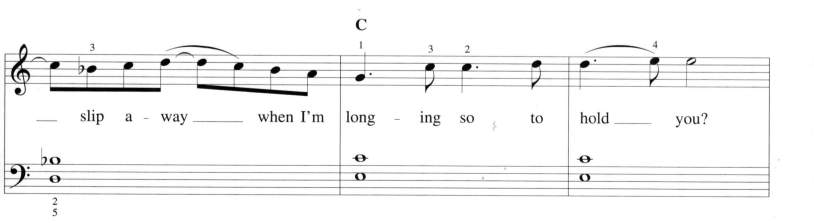

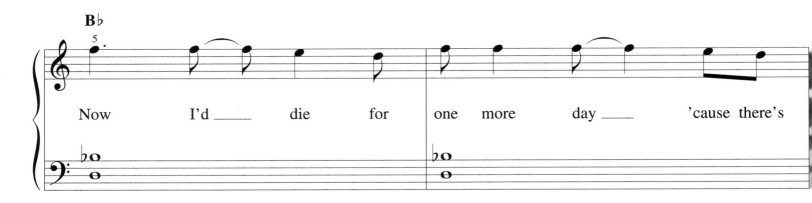

Bb

Now I'd ____ die for one more day ____ 'cause there's

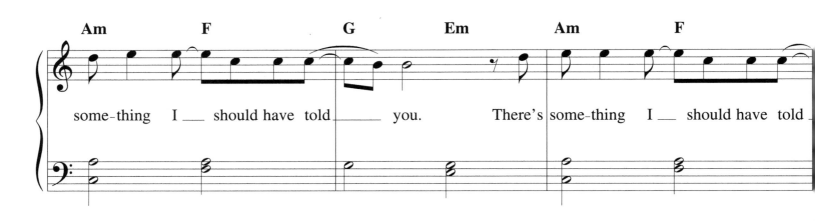

Am **F** **G** **Em** **Am** **F**

some-thing I __ should have told ____ you. There's some-thing I __ should have told

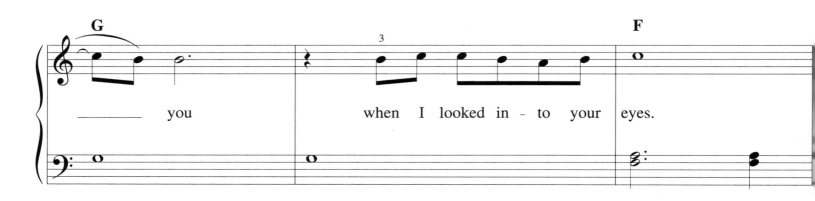

G **F**

____ you when I looked in - to your eyes.

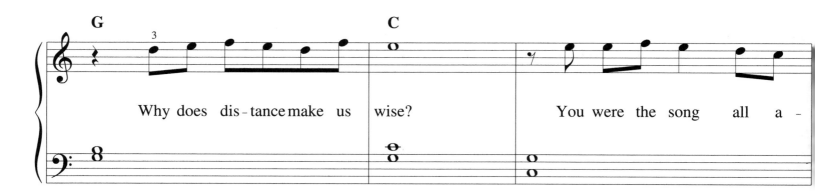

G **C**

Why does dis-tance make us wise? You were the song all a -

109

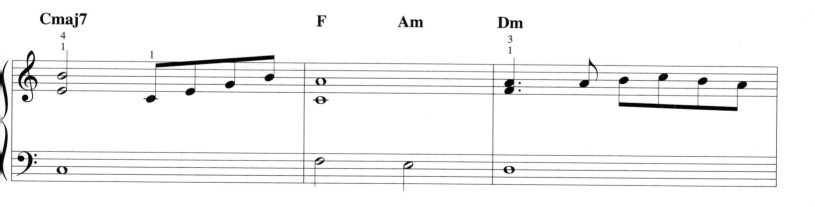

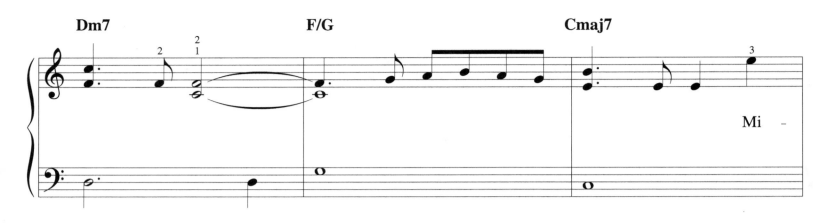

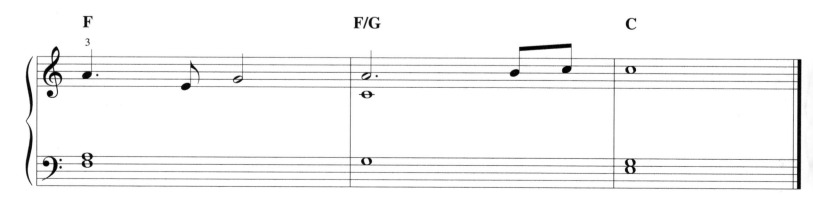